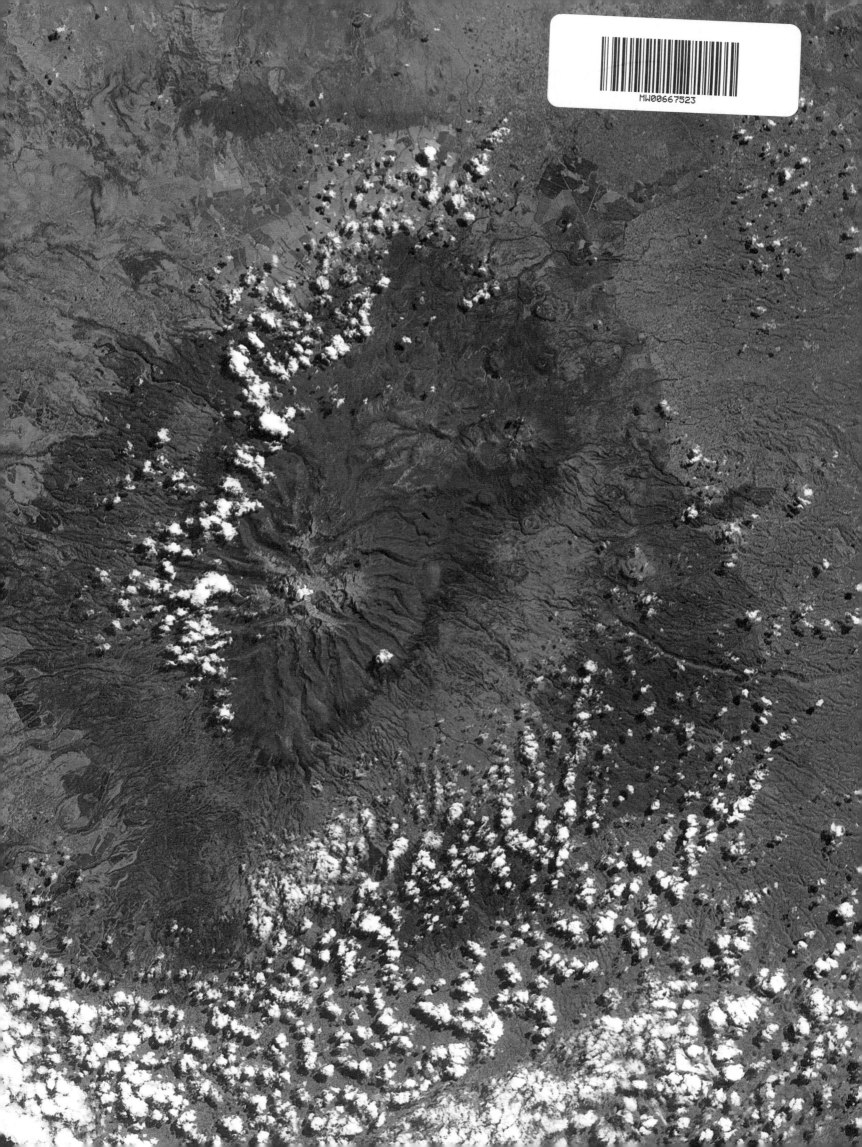

DEC 29 '95

# On God's Mountain

# On God's Mountain

**Mohamed Amin · Duncan Willetts · Brian Tetley**

Camerapix Publishers International
NAIROBI

Acknowledgements
We would like to thank James Mbugua; guides Paul Wahome and Francis Karuri; and porters Alfred Wanjohi,
Solomon Kinyua, Kahuthu Mundia, Antony Gichuki, Wainaina Abdalla, and Muriuki Nyamu, for their
companionship and mountaincraft; Captain Tad Watts, who made it possible for us to photograph Mount
Kenya from the air, and the Mountain Club of Kenya for information and research. Finally, thanks also to Phil
Snyder, Ian Howell, John Temple and John McHaffie for their invaluable suggestions and help.

First published 1991 by
Camerapix Publishers International,
P.O. Box 45048,
Nairobi, Kenya

© Camerapix 1991

ISBN 0 86190 393 5

This book was designed and produced by
Camerapix Publishers International,
P.O. Box 45048,
Nairobi, Kenya

Design: Craig Dodd

# Contents

Mountains, like men, have their history. They too are born, grow, decay and die. One cannot claim that, like men, they love, but it is true — and how true — that they are loved.
— *From No Picnic On Mount Kenya*
*by Felice Benuzzi*

End papers: Flecks of cloud cover the north and west slopes of Mount Kenya, the Nyeri district in foreground, and the north-western end of the Aberdare massif in this August 1986 satellite picture. At left, the vast Laikipia Plains, between the Aberdares and Mount Kenya, are marked by the riverine forests of the Euaso Nyro (left), born in the Abderdares, and the Naro Moru and Burguret, spawned in Mount Kenya's glaciers where they cut deep valleys on the higher slopes as they flow west. At right, the rivers born on the east and south slopes of this strategic watershed scour deep gorges and valleys through lush forests and fertile farmlands. On the mountain summit, shadowed by a solitary cloud, the peak glaciers are clearly visible while the distinctive shape of the Giant's Billiard Table and Ithinguni are at right, and (above them) Rutundu and Rutundu Tarn. Around the mountain at the top of the picture are the fertile wheatlands (left) of Timau and the distinctive coffee and tea fields (right) of Meru.

Half-title: Silhouetted against the early morning sun, a lone climber stands at the edge of the precipice that rises 1,000 feet above Lake Michaelson in the Gorges Valley, near the Temple, on the approach from Chogoria. Title Pages: Mellow sun bathes the northern moorlands that roll down from the craggy peaks of Mount Kenya at 14,000 feet. Contents Pages: Reticulated giraffe roam the sun-scorched Laikipia plains as Mount Kenya thrusts 17,058 feet into the sky astride the Equator. Pages 6–7: Treacherous crevasses in the pristine ice of the Lewis Glacier. Following pages: Lewis Glacier from Point Lenana, with the Austrian Hut in the background (centre) and Teleki Valley in centre background.

# Prologue

The message had come to Bibi Muthoni in a dream. Now she was 12,000 feet high on the moorlands of the sacred mountain, *Kere-Nyaga*. She was barefoot. Above and beyond she could make out the thrusting spires of its twin peaks covered with a mantle of snow.

She had never been here before but she knew the way. The message had been clear. *Ngai*, the Creator, the One God, who lived on the highest point of *Kere-Nyaga*, had been adamant. His peace was disturbed.

From time immemorial Muthoni's ancestors, and the Maasai, and those of the Kimeru and the Kiembu, who lived across on the other side of the mountain, had paid homage to the Lord of Nature.

The tale was told in tribal lore, handed down from generation to generation, of how at the beginning of time *Ngai*, the Divider of the Universe who created mankind, had summoned Gikuyu, the father of the tribe, and had given him his share of the land with its rivers and forests and game and all the gifts that the Lord of Nature bestowed on mankind.

And then, as a sign of his powers and his wonders, *Ngai* had made *Kere-Nyaga* his resting place.

And he took Gikuyu to the top of this mountain of mystery and pointed out, there below them, the beauty of the land which he had created and given to Gikuyu.

And he ordered Gikuyu, whenever he was in need, to make a sacrifice and to raise his hands to *Kere-Nyaga* and he, *Ngai*, would help.

Muthoni thought about the legend as she climbed still higher. She had left her *shamba*, farm, on the lower slopes before sunup. Now she was edging her way over the rocks and ice at 15,000 feet.

She had seen the place in her dream. Not far from here was the cairn of rocks that covered the bodies of three climbers who had been killed on the mountain many years before. Rescuers had built the cairn and relatives and friends had made the plaque which had been set into it.

And *Ngai* was angry.

In her dream, Muthoni had seen the grave and the plaque. Ngai had told her that no one who died on the mountain should be buried there.

And he had ordered her to climb up *Kere-Nyaga* and remove the plaque.

The grave lay very high, between 15,000 and 16,000 feet, in the steep screes at the foot of the Darwin Glacier, directly beneath the sacred peaks of Batian and Nelion.

Now, as she climbed the last few yards on the treacherous scree, deep in the lengthening shadows of day's close, the last, fading flicker of sundown bathed the twin peaks an ethereal gold.

When Muthoni reached the cairn she slowly set about removing the plaque. Finally, the deep valley now dark and icy, her work was done and she began to make her way down the mountain.

Late that night, as she walked down the mountain in darkness, a party of

Opposite: Where the tree line meets moorland at 11,000 feet on Mount Kenya, lobelia, *Deckenii keniensis*, endemic only to Mount Kenya's bogs and marshes, displays prodigious growth, rising to heights of twenty feet or more.

rangers found the simple, barefoot peasant woman clutching the plaque. When they questioned her they listened in some disbelief.

Did she know she was trespassing in a national park?

*Ngai* had sent her, she told them.

They escorted her to the park warden's house in the forest at 8,000 feet. American-born Phil Snyder listened with growing wonder as the story unfolded.

He was young and he had been brought up in California. Stories of visions and dreams were something he normally treated with cynicism. But in the mid-1970s Phil Snyder had been warden of Mount Kenya National Park for some time. He had once found a barefoot mystic with a short length of rope, a black kettle, and a tattered bible on top of Nelion, Africa's third-highest point.

He, too, had sensed something of what actress Stefanie Powers would later describe as the mountain's 'brooding presence . . . a spirit ancient and impassive, indifferent to all human concerns yet charged with unvoiced secrets'.

Muthoni had finished her work. She handed the plaque to Snyder. He told the rangers to escort her back to her *shamba*.

Snyder placed the plaque on one side. Nobody knew the mountain better or had climbed it more often. But clearly Muthoni had been given a mission and Phil Snyder had always respected *Kere-Nyaga* and its legends. He had no intention of returning the plaque to its original place.

Opposite: Mount Kenya's high moorlands are studded with enchanted jade tarns. Giant tussock grass, which covers much of Mount Kenya between the 11,000-15,000-foot contours, tests the stamina of all who walk the higher slopes of this hauntingly beautiful mountain.

Left: Rosette leaves of the water-filled lobelia protect it against high-altitude frost.

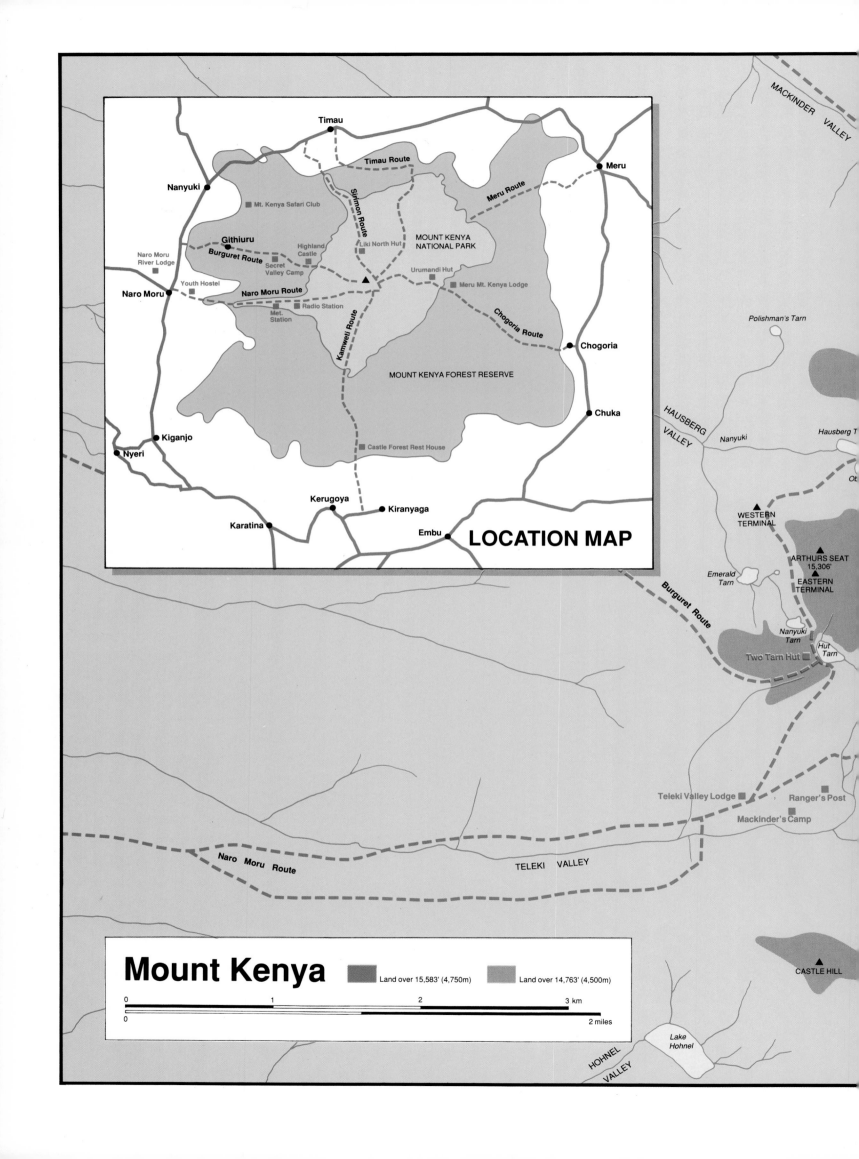

LOCATION MAP

# Mount Kenya

Land over 15,583' (4,750m)  Land over 14,763' (4,500m)

0    1    2    3 km
0                2 miles

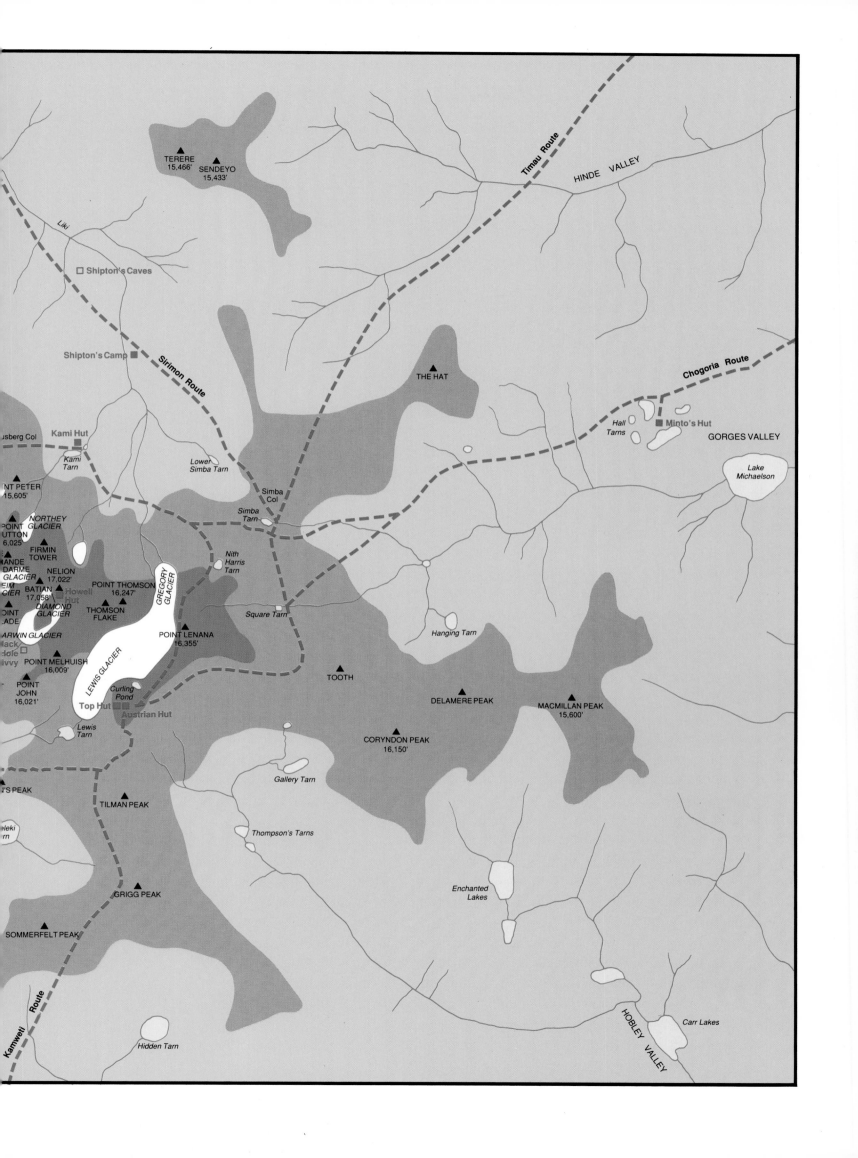

TERERE
15,466'

SENDEYO
15,433'

Liki

HINDE VALLEY

Timau Route

Sirimon Route

Chogoria Route

□ Shipton's Caves

Shipton's Camp ■

Kami Hut

THE HAT

Hall
Tarns

Minto's Hut ■

GORGES VALLEY

usberg Col

Kami
Tarn

Lower
Simba Tarn

Lake
Michaelson

NT PETER
15,605'

Simba
Col

NORTHEY
GLACIER

POINT
UTTON
6,025

Simba
Tarn

FIRMIN
TOWER

Nith
Harris
Tarn

RANDE
DARME
GLACIER

NELION
17,022'

POINT THOMSON
16,247'

GREGORY GLACIER

EIM
CIER

BATIAN
17,058'

Howell
Hut

OINT
LADE

DIAMOND
GLACIER

THOMSON
FLAKE

Square Tarn

Hanging Tarn

ARWIN GLACIER

POINT LENANA
16,355'

lack
ole
ivvy

LEWIS GLACIER

POINT MELHUISH
16,009'

TOOTH

POINT
JOHN
16,021'

Curling
Pond

DELAMERE PEAK

MACMILLAN PEAK
15,600'

Top Hut

Austrian Hut

Lewis
Tarn

CORYNDON PEAK
16,150'

S PEAK

TILMAN PEAK

Gallery Tarn

eleki
rn

Thompson's Tarns

GRIGG PEAK

Enchanted
Lakes

SOMMERFELT PEAK

HOBLEY VALLEY

Carr Lakes

Kamweti Route

Hidden Tarn

# 1 Introduction: God's Abode

To the people who live in its shadows Mount Kenya is sacred as the home of God.

The first people to settle around the mountain — at any time from between 5,000 and 10,000 years ago — were the Ndorobo. This group of hunter-gatherers, who formed one of Kenya's earliest ethnic communities, know it as 'the spotted mountain', *Doinyo Egeri*.

The nomadic Maasai, who for centuries grazed their cattle at the foot of Africa's second-highest mountain, know it as 'the striped mountain', *ol Doinyo Geri*. The Kikuyu, who settled its forested, lower slopes between 400 and 500 years ago, call it 'mountain of brightness', *Kirinyaga*, and the Wakamba, *Kiinya'a*, a corruption of the Kikuyu name.

Both the Maasai and the Kikuyu believe that God — the Kikuyu name for God is *Ngai*, the Maasai, *Engai* — has made His home on the highest point of the Mountain of Brightness.

And to the climbers who scale its twin peaks, or stand at their feet, Mount Kenya is also a holy of holies.

But although the Ndorobo and these communities were the first to make their home beneath the magnificent cathedral-like spires of Mount Kenya they were latecomers to what, even now, foot-for-foot is one of the world's great mountains. In fact, the daunting peaks that on a bright, clear day can be seen from Nairobi, 130 kilometres distant, form the eroded plug that was once lodged deep in the throat of an ice-clad cone thousands of feet higher than the 19,340-foot summit of what is now Africa's highest mountain, Kilimanjaro.

Indeed, Mount Kenya was once among the world's highest mountains — a free-standing massif that seemed to touch the sky.

But aeons of erosion, by wind, rain, and glacial disturbance, have worn away the crater rim until all that remains are the twin peaks of Batian and Nelion; yet they are still higher than any point on the European land mass. Batian reaches 17,058 feet into the Equatorial sky, and Nelion is only thirty-six feet lower. There is also a mass of subsidiary peaks almost as high and virtually as challenging to the climber.

And, no matter the wearing away of the millenniums, they testify to the grandeur that was — and still is — Mount Kenya's. It is much older than the relatively-young Kilimanjaro, which is only a million or so years old and still at its highest.

When Mount Kenya was born three, possibly ten, million years ago in a cataclysmic upheaval, it stood at least another 6,000 feet (some say 10,000 feet or more) higher than today; close, indeed, to the girt and dimensions of the giants of the Indian subcontinent.

The mountain's birth began in a series of tumultuous movements, long before the earliest ancestors of mankind evolved in the Great Rift Valley two or three million years ago, which shaped the eastern side of Africa. Arching its back in spasms of prolonged labour, eastern Africa writhed, rising and falling in drawn out convulsions.

Above: Delicate flower of Mackinder's gladiolus, *Gladiolus watsonoides*, also known as bottle flush, blooms at the edge of the 10,000-foot tree line on the ascent from Naro Moru.

Previous pages: Tendrils of mis caress the forbidding central peaks of Mount Kenya that guard its fast-diminishing glaciers. Within this century many have disappeared and others have shrunk to less than half their size.

These thrust ancient foundation rocks upwards, causing extensive lava to flow through fissures in the earth's surface and form volcanoes. In time, these shaped the dome-shaped volcanic plateaux that characterize central Ethiopia, central Kenya, and western Uganda — all three riven, in one final convulsion, by the massive flaw of the Great Rift Valley.

Other geomorphic pressures beneath the surface, nascent streams of molten magma probing for weaknesses to exploit, extended on either side of the Rift for 160 to 250 kilometres. When these rumbling streams of pent-up energy came upon a flaw in the surface the results were awesome.

In a series of earth-trembling explosions, great cones of lava burst out of the plateaux to thrust skywards. Rising ever higher, layer upon layer, each intermittent explosion built Mount Kenya until, at its apogee, the rim of its crater stood at least 23,000 feet (and possibly 27,000 feet) above sea level and its base had a circumference of just over 300 kilometres.

And when the tremors faded and died, over millions of years the rain and the sun gave flesh to Mount Kenya's bare lava bones. Across its lower slopes lay a sensuous skin of rich, loamy soil, out of which sprang lush forests of podocarpus, cedar, hagenia, and bamboo. Higher up, a mantle of peat, bog, and strange and exotic plants spread over the mountain's skeleton.

Higher still, came layers of snow that formed deep beds of ice flowing down from the summit. Through the millenniums, this glaciation and the jet streams — sometimes lashing out in their fury at more than 200 kilometres an hour — wore away at the mountain's crumbling crater rim until only the volcano's central core remained.

There, then, came mankind's earliest ancestors to gaze in awe and wonder at this monolith in the sky. Yet, even as mankind learned to walk upright on the shores of Lake Turkana, not far distant from its icy glaciers, and spread out across the new-born savannah grasslands of the plains beneath its summit, the dying forces that gave birth to Mount Kenya were still at work. As recently as 40,000 years ago, they burst forth to create the Nyambeni hills which lie on its north-eastern flanks.

Finally, Kenya's first immigrants moved southward along the Red Sea from Egypt, through Sudan and Ethiopia, to colonise this new land in a 10,000-year-long epoch.

Distorted time and again in the retelling, and without hope of corroboration, word spread back along the line of migrants of the mantles of snow that lay upon the great mountains on and around the Equator — the Ruwenzori, Mount Elgon, Mount Kenya, and Kilimanjaro. It became part of a repository of Middle Eastern folklore about unknown Africa that, from the time of the Pharaohs to the birth of Christ, was richly embroidered with both fantasy and fact.

The wise men of Egypt, and of Greece and Rome, could only speculate on the source of the Nile, the world's longest river, whose seasonal floods and bounty of fertile silt sustained so much life. It is still an open question whether these

ancients really knew of the everlasting snow and ice on the Equator. But they certainly believed in their existence.

The second-century geographer, Ptolemy of Alexandria, stated that the Nile had its source in two great lakes fed by waters from the 'Mountains of the Moon' (history proved him right: the headwaters of the Nile rise in the Ruwenzori and flow into Lake Victoria and Lake Albert).

Aristotle wrote of the 'silver mountains' in which the Nile was born, and images of the Nile 'nourished by eternal snow' occur frequently in Latin poetry. In much the same fashion, Arab geographers, too, postulated about the source of the Nile.

But the immigrants who moved steadily southward through these many centuries — culminating in the last 1,000 years with the arrival of the Maasai and then the Kikuyu — had no need of legends or myths to fire their imaginations. On a clear day, Mount Kenya was visible for hundreds of kilometres from every direction but the west, where it lay hidden behind the Aberdare massif. Its massive flanks, rising to its almost ethereal, pyramid peaks, dominated the highland plateau east of the Rift Valley.

Nomadic pastoralists, the Maasai exploited the open grasslands on the plains below its slopes as pastures for their herds. Cultivators, the secretive Kikuyu carved smallholdings out of the forests and their glades on the lower slopes, the two communities living close together in uneasy and often acrimonious symbiosis.

But both worshipped God, the Creator, *Ngai*, as the maker of the universe and both believed that man was born atop the great mountain. According to the Kikuyu he also created *Kirinyaga* — 'mountain of brightness' — as a sign of his power as a miracle-maker and as his abode.

Their folklore tells how *Ngai* ordered Gikuyu to go to the 'tree of the building site', Mukuruene wa Nya-Gathanga, a grove of sacred wild figs, near what is now Murang'a, at a place called Mugeka, and marry Mumbi, the mother of all the Kikuyu. Mumbi raised nine daughters, who became the matriarchs of the nine Kikuyu clans.

Close kin of the Kikuyu, the Embu who live on Mount Kenya's eastern slopes, also revered the peaks as the sacred home of *Ngai*, unapproachable and ready to punish whoever dared trespass on His realm. Moreover, both Kikuyu and Embu, and their other kin, the Meru, believed that some of the rocks, rivers, and forests, were the home of evil spirits. For many of the Meru, too, the moorland lakes and forest groves were — and still are — sacred.

The Maasai also worshipped *Engai* as the dispenser of cattle and weather — rain and sunshine — in equitable proportion. So much a part of their faith is Mount Kenya that Halford Mackinder, the first European to climb to its summit, named the three highest peaks, Batian, Nelion, and Lenana, after three of the Maasai's last great nineteenth-century *laibons*, seers and medicine men who ruled the tribe.

Unforgiving and vengeful, *Kirinyaga*, has reaped terrible retribution from those seeking to intrude on this sanctuary: by the end of 1987 Mount Kenya had claimed a total of at least sixty-four lives. Though seemingly benign and benevolent when viewed from a distance early on a fine day, 'God's Mountain' can be baleful and malevolent.

There's more than just a touch of fancy to the sensations and emotions climbers experience at extremely high altitude. After all, in both Asia and Africa, they are intruding into the 'Abode of God' where mysticism must surely prevail over cynicism.

In solitude, Reinhold Messner has experienced this mysticism frequently on the peaks of major mountains. During his 1982 ascent of the world's third-highest mountain, Kanchenjunga, his perception was profound. 'First, I learned in dreams during the climb and afterwards [that] . . . the whole dream world changes for a while. . . .

'And second, I found that you see certain things between dreaming and not dreaming because you don't really sleep. . . . In the last camp near the summit, I had a very strange vision of all the human parts I am made of . . . not only of my body, but of my whole being.'

The mystique of mountain climbing has never been rationalised. The risks are incalculable and success achieves nothing of a scientific or creative value. George Mallory, who vanished with his companion Andrew Irvine during a 1924 attempt on Everest, explained his reason for putting his life on the line simply 'because it's there.'

Is that why men take the unforgiving risk? Perhaps so.

Joe Tasker, who died with his colleague Peter Boardman in 1982 on the north-east ridge of Everest, wrote that '. . . the mountains are never conquered; they will always remain and sometimes they will take away our friends if not ourselves. The climbing game is a folly, taken more or less seriously, an indulgence in an activity which is of no demonstrable benefit to anyone. It used to be that mountaineers sought to give credence to their wish to climb mountains by concealing their aims behind a shield of scientific research. But no more. It is now accepted, though not understood, that people are going to climb for its own sake.'

In a 1985 expedition on the same face, climber Sandy Allan, quoted in Andrew Greig's *Kingdoms of Experience,* soliloquised, 'Here, we're here, I'm here, hoping that my ability and the rest of the lads' ability and the gods will see us OK. We're gamblers, we've got no cash; we have lives, we love them, that's the stake.'

Thus stood, and still stands, Mount Kenya.

Opposite: Early morning sun and shadow on the summit of Nelion.

# 2 Snow on the Equator

Little more than a century ago the claim that snow existed on the Equator in East Africa sparked a long, embittered argument, a controversy that was sustained, with derision and insult, for more than thirty years. The first Europeans to see Africa's highest mountains — good Christian missionaries, honest and true — were not believed. Their claims thus dismissed, they were discredited and ridiculed by eminent geographers in Britain and Europe.

The greatest opponent was William Desborough Cooley, a man who spent most of his geographic career bound to an armchair in the Royal Geographic Society or his favourite gentlemen's club, the Athenaeum — a distance, let it be noted, of more than 5,000 kilometres from the wilderness on which he was so great an expert — debating the inaccuracies and omissions of their reports and pouring forth on the heads of these resolute men the literary equivalent of boiling oil.

Omissions and inaccuracies indeed there were; scarcely surprising for men trained not as geographers or surveyors but to preach the word of God. No map of the East African hinterland existed at all — other than those drawn centuries earlier which were based entirely on fantasy and speculation.

There are more blank spaces than physical features on Swiss missionary Johannes Rebmann's 'imperfect sketch map of East Africa' drawn in 1850. But the detail that is there is remarkable. It places Mount Kenya (he spelt it Kenia) two degrees south of the Equator. Perhaps of more significance was the fact that Rebmann suggested it was the source of the Nile.

The map caused a furore in Europe. Rebmann was mocked and derided. Not for the two degree latitudinal error — the Equator actually cuts across Mount Kenya's northern slopes at 11,500 feet, seventeen kilometres from the highest point, 17,058-foot-high Batian peak — but for his unqualified presumption in asserting that there was snow on the Equator.

Rebmann, the first European known to have seen Africa's highest mountain, 19,340-foot-high Kilimanjaro, on 11 May, 1848, came to the Church Missionary Society base in Mombasa, established some years earlier by Johann Ludwig Krapf, in 1845.

But despite his excellent map Rebmann was not the first European to see Mount Kenya. That privilege was reserved for his colleague Krapf. Late in 1849 — the year that the height of Mount Everest, the world's highest mountain, was first measured scientifically — thirty-nine-year-old Krapf travelled to the land of the Wakamba, north-west of Kilimanjaro. On 10 November he confirmed Rebmann's 'discovery' of Kilimanjaro and just over three weeks later, on 3 December, saw his first and only glimpse of Mount Kenya. He was more than 140 kilometres away — on top of a hill above the village of Kitui.

Frequently wreathed in veils of mist and cloud, Mount Kenya shies from revealing its glories. Krapf's glimpse was brief: the clouds parted only for a few minutes, just long enough for him to make out the glistening necklace of glaciers that encircle the twin peaks of Batian and Nelion.

Previous pages: Sunrise over North Liki Valley.

He described it well, though; depicting its lower buttress as 'an enormous mountain' over which rose two 'large horns or pillars'. No one, he was told, would go up the mountain because of the intense cold produced by a mysterious white substance known to the Kamba as *kirira*.

Now the storm which had greeted Rebmann's description of Kilimanjaro's snow-crested peak turned and swept over Krapf. 'The evidence in the case of this more accessible mountain [Kilimanjaro] was far more definite,' wrote J. W. Gregory in *The Great Rift Valley*, an entertaining account of his 1892 geological survey, 'and it is therefore not surprising that Krapf's story was discredited, in spite of his description of the appropriate emotions that overcame him.'

The so-called learned geographers in London dismissed Krapf's eyewitness account and said that what he had taken for snow was nothing more than 'calcareous earth' — in other words, chalk. Embittered and angered by the prevailing cynicism of Cooley and his cronies at the Royal Geographical Society, including the President, Sir Roderick Murchison — who thought such facts 'to a great degree incredulous' and therefore only fanciful — Krapf determined to establish his veracity and in 1851 he retraced his steps to Kitui and beyond, coming some sixty or so kilometres closer to Mount Kenya.

But the mountain remained hidden; perhaps fittingly so (if unfairly to him) for a mountain that had been revered as sacred for so long. Krapf had no second chance. He was forced to retreat after his small caravan was attacked by a Kamba raiding party on the banks of the Tana River the headwaters of which, ironically, sprang out of Mount Kenya's glaciers.

Eighteen years later another European, the botanist J. M. Hildebrandt, collected plant specimens around Kitui but he records no mention of the mountain and, presumably, did not see it.

Krapf died a disappointed man in 1881, thirty-two years after that fateful December day in 1849, denied the vindication he so justly deserved. It was to be another two years before Mount Kenya was seen by a European for the second time. This honour fell to Joseph Thomson, a young Scotsman, commissioned by the Royal Geographical Society, under Murchison's successor Lord Aberdare, to establish the truth or otherwise of snow on the Equator.

Spurning Stanley's advice to take a thousand men or die, Thomson marched up from the Kenya coast through Maasailand, to Lake Naivasha, the highest and purest of the seven Rift Valley lakes in Kenya. To the east it is dominated by one of Kenya's greatest mountain massifs, Nyandarua, its highest point, Lesatima, reaching more than 13,000 feet above sea level.

These mountain moorlands, a forty-six-kilometre-long north-south plateau stretching between Lesatima and Kinangop, the second-highest point at 12,815 feet, so reminded Joseph Thomson of his Scottish heath that he named them the Aberdares after the President of the Royal Geographical Society. He assumed, wrongly, that it was not one mountain but a range of mountains.

And it was from Naivasha, late in 1883, that Thomson with Brahim, his

Zanzibari gunbearer, trudged up through the rime-covered giant tussock heather, wary of the belligerent buffalo and elephant that still roam these heights, to marvel, on a glorious day in the glow of a false dawn, a few minutes before the sun exploded into light behind the mountain and began its swift climb to its zenith, at the scene which greeted him at the top.

'Through a rugged and picturesque depression of the range [the Aberdares] rose a gleaming snow-white peak with sparkling facets, which scintillated with the superb beauty of a colossal diamond. It was, in fact, the very image of a great crystal or sugar loaf. At the base of this beautiful peak were two small excrescences like supporters of a monument. From these, at a very slight angle, shaded away a long glittering white line, seen above the mass of the Aberdare range like the silver lining of a dark storm-cloud. This peak and silvery line formed the central culmination of Mount Kenya.

'As I stood entranced at this fulfilment of my dearest hopes, I drew a great sigh of satisfaction and as I said to Brahim: "Look!" and pointed to the glittering crystal, I am not sure but there was something like a tear in my eye. But now, even while I stood and gazed, a moisture laden breeze touched the peak, wove a fleecy mantle and gradually enshrouded the heaven-like spectacle. In a few moments there but remained a bank of clouds over the wood. But I beheld a vision as if from the Unseen to lure me on.'

Thus did Thomson get his first glimpse of Africa's second-highest point, its twin spires thrusting into the sky above the Equator, with the Diamond Glacier like a jewel at its throat.

He should have seen more. But though he strived, Thomson was unable to reach even the mountain's lower, forested slopes. His trail from Thomson's Falls, now Nyahururu, across the Laikipia Plains, was barred by the fearsome Maasai.

Nonetheless, virtually self-educated, from a distance of eighty kilometres, he gave not only a lyrical and accurate description of the mountain but also identified correctly the origins of its peaks as the plug which ended its volcanic life. Ironically, though he was only the second European known to have seen the mountain, the only single feature of Mount Kenya which bears his name (a point between Nelion and Point Lenana) was given, in fact, in honour of John Thomson, a geographer of the Royal Geographical Society, long after Joseph Thomson had returned to Britain.

And so, although during the 1880s many successfully explored Kilimanjaro, even reaching its summit and identifying its unique flora and fauna, Mount Kenya remained, to all intents and purposes, as much of an enigma as it had been after Krapf first saw it. It was left to another European, following four years behind Thomson, to shed the light — and some may say confusion — of first-hand experience on the sacred mountain of the Maasai and the Kikuyu.

Transylvanian nobleman Count Samuel Teleki von Szek was one of those Victorian aristocrats fortunate enough to possess both the means and the health to indulge in travel to unknown places. In 1886 he planned a long expedition into

29

the East African hinterland and after reading a beseeching appeal from one Lieutenant Ludwig von Hohnel, who had heard of his plans, he appointed the Austrian naval officer his aide.

Landing on the mainland in January 1887, the expedition reached the slopes of Mount Kenya early in October and on 17 October, after much preparation, and with four guides and forty porters — leaving von Hohnel behind somewhere in the vicinity of Kiganjo and Naro Moru — Teleki began the first known ascent of the mountain's high reaches.

Though all this happened just over a century ago, it's difficult now to understand the immense challenge that this expedition represented. The mountain forests were alive with wild — and dangerous — game. No trails, save those made by the elephant, cut through the ancient timber giants and bamboo belt which swathed the mountain between the 7,000 and 12,000 foot contours. And, even though it was only 100 years ago, the snowline was also much lower and more extensive.

The weather, too, was inclement: the short rains that fall in Kenya between October and November had set in. But while von Hohnel on the plains below marvelled over 'woods and fields, which had been so dry and dreary-looking . . . bursting everywhere with fresh life and clothed with vivid green', Teleki and his party were shivering under the icy grip of the heavy clouds that continuously shrouded the mountain.

'Masses of snow, extending far down the slopes, betrayed what the state of things must be on the heights,' records von Hohnel. 'All these made me very anxious for the Count's return. . . .'

Fortunately, his anxiety was unjustified. Eight days after the expedition set out, Teleki returned with tales of the many wonderful things that he had experienced during his climb — first meeting plentiful game on the approach 'through woods denser than those lower down', but not so dense as those on Kilimanjaro 'though the trees were taller', to the point where the climb steepened.

Indeed, Teleki and his party had found the going surprisingly easy and were soon upon the thick and impenetrable bamboo belt that characterises Mount Kenya between the 8,000 and 10,000 foot contours. But it would have been 'quite impassable if a path had not been trodden through them by elephants and buffaloes'.

Even so, they found 'to use the axe and to part the bamboo stems, dripping wet with rain', with their outstretched arms was exhausting work. Teleki established his camp at what he estimated was around 8,600 feet, amid an abundance of wildlife — colobus monkeys 'and a leopard which suddenly announced its presence with a growl quite close to us, only however to disappear in the thicket again immediately'. Vividly-coloured game birds and parrots broke the silence with their shrill cries.

All next day the party had to hack its way through the bamboo. 'The higher we got the thicker grew the stems, and the more arduous was the work of forcing a passage.'

Now the bamboo thinned out but other barriers arose — an eighteen-foot-wide stream among them — and by noon, exhausted, Teleki made camp again at the upper level of the bamboo, estimating his height at about 10,000 feet (how lucky today's climber who can climb a well-made all-weather road by car or foot to the weather station at the same altitude on the ridge of the valley which Teleki followed).

So dense was the mist, and so persistent the rain, that Teleki took all his bearings by compass alone but when the party set out the following morning on 20 October, 1887, he noticed that the 'ascent became noticeably steeper'. Leaving the bamboo behind almost at once, after climbing 500 feet the forest began to clear, too.

Teleki was now somewhere near the foot of what is today called 'the vertical bog', a stamina-sapping exercise in tedious exhaustion which clogs the feet every inch of the climb for the next 1,500 to 2,000 feet. But he was pleasantly distracted from this ordeal by the strange growth of the exotic alpine flora that now replaced the trees — giant forms of the lobelias which in European conditions are dwarf plants.

Some of these high-altitude mutations are found only on Kenya, other species

and subspecies only on Kilimanjaro. Their highest points separated by 320 kilometres, both mountains boast their own unique ecosystems though they share many common features.

The weather was abysmal: it rained continuously and the temperature was barely above freezing, 8°C. At noon, with the men 'grey and shivering with cold', Teleki decided to make camp again, this time at an estimated height of 11,600 feet. While the men set up camp, Teleki went on ahead to survey the route. 'I found that the course we had taken had by no means been badly chosen, as we had reached the base of the loftiest peak of the mountain'.

In fact, he was probably a good deal higher (and therefore Mount Kenya a good deal lower) than he estimated. A map drawn a few years later by J. W. Gregory, only the second man to climb to the base of the peaks, indicates Teleki's camp as 2,200 feet higher than the Hungarian estimated. If he was near the head of the valley that bears his name this would be right. Teleki Lodge, built recently near the site of the camp set up by Halford J. Mackinder, who followed Teleki thirteen years later, is 14,200 feet above sea level. Teleki's aneroid may have given him the wrong altitude readings but his own account leaves little doubt that he was some way up the valley, if not actually at its head.

Whether his estimates of altitude were right or wrong, what seems most remarkable a century later is that the route which he chose at random, without hindsight of any previous experience, is now by far the most frequently used of any of the six major routes on the mountain.

'Further up I came to many perpendicular precipices, but I always found room to climb between them. The slopes were, in many places, dotted with remarkable isolated column-like pieces of rock sixty to 160 feet high.'

Teleki was delighted when one of his expedition leaders, Mahommed Seiff, brought him a nest containing a fledgling of a species of Nectarinia (subsequently named Nectarinia deckeni by a Vienna ornithologist, after Baron von der Decken, who explored Kilimanjaro in 1862-63, later being murdered on the Juba River during an 1865 expedition intended to confirm Krapf's discovery of Mount Kenya). The numbers of this bird that the aristocrat saw at this height — 'ten or twelve appearing at once' — were, he noted, remarkable.

Next morning, he left camp hoping to climb much higher but was forced back by fog and rain and had to wait until the following day, 22 October, 1887, to set off again; which he did at four in the morning. Some time later he and his barefoot party of twelve had reached a height that he estimated at 13,600 feet, the edge of existence on Mount Kenya.

Having passed a rock hyrax, the highest-living mammal on Mount Kenya — which he describes as a 'tailless marmot' — it is almost certain that he was some way above the vicinity of what would become Mackinder's Camp. It was 7°C and his barefoot companions were 'suffering terribly from cold'. He decided to continue alone but Mahommed Seiff insisted on accompanying him.

After climbing another 1,000 feet or more, the two reached the snowline

35

Opposite: Mount Kenya seen
from a ridge of the Teleki Valley
on the Naro Moru ascent.

beneath which lay hardened ice — only for Teleki to realise that he had taken the wrong ridge to reach the summit. 'From where I stood, however, I could tell that we could have only done so with very great difficulty, the bank on that side rising perpendicularly to a height of some 300 to 450 feet. An equally deep ravine which would, however, have been easier to scale, and part of the wall of the crater alone separated me now from the crater itself, but as that wall was lower than where I stood, my view was not interrupted.'

From the description that then follows of what is now known as the Lewis Glacier and Teleki Tarn, at the eastern foot of Shipton's Peak, it seems that the Austrian aristocrat was standing on the crest of the 14,800-foot-high ridge that guards Teleki Valley in the south. The reading on his aneroid placed him at 15,355 feet above sea level — a difference of 500 feet or so.

He was the first European to see Batian and Nelion from close range and, although he wrongly deduced that Mount Kenya was an extant volcano surrounded by a crater, his description of its appearance cannot be faulted.

'On my left rose the rugged peak of Kenia, all that was left of the original cone. From its steep sides quantities of ice most often roll down to form the chaotic masses piled up at its base. The columnar-like phonolithic rock of the highest peak is of a light-brown colour, and the actual peak is split and rises up in two pillars.'

Next day, well pleased with his adventure, Teleki began the descent to Ndoro and von Hohnel. And although his observations of the flora and wildlife earned commendation, his conclusion that he had seen a crater wall — and his subsequent assumptions about the mountain's geology — was described, some years later, as less than satisfactory.

But in 1887 there was nobody to argue for he had been where no other European had. Nor would he soon be followed. In the next three or four years others did attempt to emulate him but failed: among them were J. R. W. Piggott who penetrated close enough in 1889 to study the mountain's face; and the British East Africa expedition of 1891 led by Captain F. G. Dundas, with Bird Thompson and C. W. Hobley.

The expedition attempted to cut through the south-eastern forests, the thickest and oldest on the mountain and found them virtually impenetrable, reaching only to a height of between 8,000 and 9,000 feet and giving Hobley a glimpse that led him to form the wrong impression that the mountain was 'more properly a mountain-chain and not a single mountain. . . .'

The German colonialist Carl Peters, who was eager to annexe Kenya as a German colony had also been around its slopes and photographed the mountain. His pictures gave some indication of the difficulties any potential climber had to face.

It remained for John Walter Gregory, another Briton of the same ilk as Thomson, to conduct the first serious study of the mountain's geology, and flora and fauna. The main thrust of Gregory's 1892-93 expedition, however, was to investigate the geology of the Rift Valley. This traumatic flaw, 'so different from anything else on the surface of the earth', that stretches more than 6,000 kilometres from Russia to Mozambique, fascinated Gregory who found it natural to ask whether it had all been formed at the same time by the same process.

It was to satisfy his 'desire to obtain more precise geological information' about the Rift Valley's structure that Gregory journeyed to East Africa late in 1892. A major, but secondary, purpose was to explore Mount Kenya. He was given a great deal of support in this enterprise by Piggott who was the administrator of the Imperial British East Africa (IBEA) company.

Gregory had already done his work on the Rift at Baringo — chiselling out samples of the different strata of rock that would prove conclusively how the Rift was formed — when squabbling between the resident Ilchamus fisherfolk, also known as Njemps, some coastal traders, and the Tuken warriors from the hills above, made him decide it was time to move.

He pondered four courses of action: returning directly along the Rift Valley to Fort Smith at Kabete, near what was to become Nairobi; striking west to Uganda and the Ruwenzori; travelling northward to Basso Narok, now Lake Turkana; or crossing the Laikipia Plateau, where the formidable, warring Maasai held sway, to climb Kenya.

Gregory came close to abandoning this last plan. 'The objections to this,' he records, 'were twofold: there was the possibility that Mr. Astor Chanler and Lieut. von Hohnel [Teleki's erstwhile companion was making an attempt on the mountain from the east that subsequently ended before he reached it] had already worked out the structure of that mountain; and there was the certainty of trouble with the Masai if I met them.'

Against these arguments, he concluded, was the fact that it was his original plan to explore the mountain. 'I had started intending to go to Kenya, and so to Kenya I resolved to go.' As a scientist and explorer, he had good reason to make this decision.

Kilimanjaro, he notes, had been ascended to the summit, geologically mapped, and its flora and fauna described in some detail. 'In regard to Kenya, however, our knowledge was most rudimentary.'

As well as confused nineteenth-century estimates about its height, varying from 18,000 feet to 23,000 feet, there was also the argument about whether it was a well-preserved crater or a volcano in the last stages of decay. Almost nothing was known about the mountain. Teleki never took the voluminous notes on ethnography, fauna, and flora that his companion von Hohnel so assiduously recorded, and his literary sketch of Mount Kenya is brief indeed, leaving almost everything to the imagination.

Gregory was now resolved to settle once and for all the many mysteries and speculations surrounding the mountain. Not without personal danger. Apart from the risk of encountering the Maasai on his march across the Laikipia — and he was the only European in his party — there were many hazards to face when

Above: One of Mount Kenya's endemic species of rodent.

he began to climb upward, of which nobody was more aware than Gregory.

'I assured every one on the coast [before his departure upcountry] that I had no intention of completing the ascent; for I guessed from Peters' photograph that it was not likely to yield to anyone climbing alone, and none of the Zanzibari [his porters] could be expected to venture upon the snow.'

Thus he set out from Baringo and, after crossing the Laikipia, skirted the north-western face of the mountain 'at a sufficient distance from the base . . . to get a general view. . . . At noon we selected the bay of moorland that seemed to run highest into the forests, and at its head chose a place for camp'.

Gregory was in much the same position as Teleki, and the British East Africa expedition that followed. Their attempt to climb the mountain from the south failed almost at its outset, when they turned back on the lower slopes unable to penetrate the thicker forests that grew above the Embu-Kirinyaga-Kerugoya district. Although all this had taken place some time before, a brief note of their experiences had been published only as Gregory was preparing to leave England.

For his base camp the geologist moved a few hundred feet up the mountain and spent the day in hectic preparation for his ascent. 'Loads were re-sorted, rations served out for ten days and reserve food packed. Twice Omari [Gregory's headman] and I went through the baggage, to pick out things that could possibly be left behind. My own kit was cut down to the lowest possible limit, though I took all available clothing to lend to the men.'

For those in the 1980s who gaily hurry up and down the mountain in the span of two or three days, a perspective of time and place may help an appreciation of Gregory's position. He was attempting to reach a point higher than any ground in Europe, in a country that was still little known, where the vagaries and predictability, or otherwise, of the climate were unrecorded, and where only one European had been before.

Three decades later, a Scottish missionary, the Reverend J. W. Arthur, told an audience at the Royal Geographical Society in London, 'The difficulties with which these earlier explorers were faced were formidable, not only from the want of knowledge of the climatic conditions of the mountain, but also from the unsettled state of the native tribes, who were engaged in constant inter-tribal warfare, making it dangerous for Europeans to intrude into their country.'

But Gregory did not intend to take any unnecessary risks. Even as he and the men worked, a clammy mist clamped down on them obscuring all visibility, only dispersing for a few brief minutes at sundown. Nonetheless, the break was long enough to allow Gregory to take a bearing on the summit and study the direction of the valleys and ridges leading to it — enabling him to plan his route through the forests and across the moorlands. He chose to ascend a valley to the south of that taken by Teleki; it may have been Thego Valley the one next to Hohnel Valley.

Early next morning the men were paraded. Gregory handpicked twelve to

accompany him and started at once for the summit — Omari leading and Gregory following in the rearguard to hustle along any dawdlers and thwart would-be deserters. He had reason. Some of the porters he had chosen in Zanzibar had been in the British East Africa expedition and had told 'such pitiful tales of their sufferings, that the porters were loth to enter the dreaded forests'.

They had not exaggerated their fears. Gregory's route through the forests was much more daunting than that taken by Teleki and, moreover, the party was shrouded almost continuously in mist, which saturated everything. Cutting through the bamboo, which grew forty foot high and was packed so closely together it was often impossible to force a way between, was the most trying work Gregory had ever experienced.

'Through this dark and dismal forest,' he writes, 'we had to force a way. Occasionally an elephant path would run in our direction, and we could then make comparatively rapid progress, delaying only to lop off the lower branches of the bamboos, to cut through fallen stems, or to climb over dead tree trunks. The elephants, however, did not obey the rules of mountaineering and their tracks soon ran down into the valleys, so that most of the way we had to cut a path step by step. Every blow of our mattocks upon the bamboos shook the sodden canopy overhead, and continual shower-baths of water kept us wet and miserable. My clothes were soaked through, while the raw, damp cold chilled the porters to the marrow. We had to stop every hour to light fires to warm them, and even then they found the climate almost unbearable, and one or two cried like children.' These were not upcountry Kikuyu or Maasai but men whose families had for centuries been reared in the humid warmth of the Indian Ocean coast or the island of Zanzibar.

Gregory had planned to climb above the forests in two days but on the night of the second he realised this was impossible. His disappointment was even more intense when he checked the boiling-point thermometers by which he measured the altitude and discovered that they had only risen 1,700 feet, despite all their labour and suffering. By the next night he was even more disconsolate.

'The bamboos were as thick as ever. We were so exhausted that, when the order to camp was given, we all lay down where we stood. . . . We had not once seen or felt the sun since we left the meadows of Laikipia. We had never once seen more than twenty yards ahead, and it was only rarely that we could see up to the tree tops. The natural history had also been disappointing. Of vegetation there was enough and to spare; but the species were few, and the plants so sodden with moisture that I could not press them; the bamboos were especially irritating, for I could not find a single flower or fruit, and thus it had been impossible to determine the genus to which they belong. Many animals were not to be expected, and we saw only one pack of monkeys, some red-breasted birds rather larger than robins, many slugs and snails, and a few insects. At night we heard the shrill cry of a cony (*Procavia shoana*, Gigl. [it was in fact a tree hyrax, *Dendrohyrax*, of the same family]), of which I found a skull.'

Little wonder, perhaps, that some years earlier in circumstances like these, or maybe even more extreme, Hobley and his companions abandoned their attempt to break through the forest. But Gregory's persistence was to be rewarded. Next day, at around noon, the party emerged from the bamboo into the warmth of the Equatorial sun.

'The forests gave place to scattered clumps of trees, and the rank undergrowth to a firm rich turf. . . . The men threw down their loads and basked in the sunshine, while I examined the sections in the stream banks, and collected the flowers on the meadows. Many of these were old friends.'

He discovered dandelion, clover, blackberries, and bitter-cress, and stumbled over the first of the exotic giants of dwarf alpines that flourish at high altitudes on the Equator, 'Some silvery gray bushes about six feet in height, which clothed the hillside . . . an arborescent form of that most typical of Alpine meadow plants, the Lady's Mantle, (*Alchemilla*)'.

These were mingled with gladiolus, which Gregory had not seen in the wild before, and 'others, such as a tree-lobelia, which were of a type quite new to me. I also caught some specimens of a common English butterfly, the Clouded Yellow (*Colias edusa*, Linn)'.

But the relief was brief. It was the end of June, but the climate was at its worst and the bogs and swamps near impassable. Soon the clouds descended and the expedition was struck by the equivalent of a tropical blizzard — a raging gale of hail and sleet.

Under this onslaught, as Gregory climbed on ahead looking for a place to camp, the men collapsed on the icy, half-frozen peat bog. The following day Gregory established a base camp in a drier, more protected area and then moved up another 1,500 to 1,750 feet to set up the camp from which he would explore the peak area.

'We had to march for some time across a peat bog, over which we made fair progress, until the crust thawed; after this we were for most of the time plunged up to the waist in half-frozen peat.' Finally he found a spot amid some crags of agglomerate close to a grove of giant groundsel and lobelia where his men begged to stop. Gregory 'was only too willing to grant their request'. After making camp, most returned to the base lower down — only Gregory, his personal attendant, Fundi Mbaruk, a cook, and one porter too weak to walk, remaining behind.

It was from this camp that Gregory conducted the first comprehensive survey of the mountain and its glaciers; a scientific summary of which appeared in Britain's *Geographical Journal* and the *Quarterly Journal* of the Geological Society. He is responsible for many of the names which characterise the valleys and peaks of Mount Kenya.

'As it is impossible to describe the mountain without names,' he wrote, 'some have had to be invented. I should not, of course, think of applying European terms to places for which native names are already in existence; but in a locality

Right: Leopard proliferate in Mount Kenya's benign and protected ancient rainforests, often making forays high up the mountain to the snow line and beyond.

Right: Kenya's endangered rhino, with less than 500 remaining at the end of the 1980s, have held out in the sanctuary of Mount Kenya and its rainforests for thousands of years.

where there are no names, there can be no reasonable objection to proposing them.'

Propose he did, and with comprehensive vigour — starting with Teleki's Valley and Teleki Tarn, hidden by Shipton's Peak; Thomson Valley, north of Teleki Valley, after the Scottish explorer (the name didn't stick and it's now known as Hausberg Valley after Mackinder's companion); Hohnel Valley and at its head, Lake Hohnel and 15,800-foot-high Mount Hohnel (because of a drawing of this feature made on the plains below by 'this accomplished cartographer'); Teleki Ridge, leading to Point Lenana; Hobley Valley, which that expedition would have followed if it had made it through the forests to the south, and at its head two tarns named Thompson's tarns, after the leader of Hobley's expedition; Point Piggott after the incumbent administrator of the IBEA; the Lewis Glacier, after Professor Henry Carvell Lewis 'whose brilliant researches have thrown so much light on glacial problems'; the Tyndall Glacier, after John Tyndall, the famous physicist and alpinist; the Darwin Glacier, 'so named as we owe to Darwin the first precise description of a glacial valley in England'; and the Heim and Forel Glaciers, after two Swiss geologists, because they were 'very useful' survey points. Initially, in his original *Geographical Journal* articles, the Tyndall and Darwin glaciers were juxtaposed but he switched them around later when he wrote his book. Gregory's spellings, too, were inconsistent.

Of the many excursions he made from this camp, Gregory rated his climb of Mount Hohnel — its western face composed of a series of almost vertical lava cliffs — as the most interesting. 'The snow on the ledges was in a very unstable condition, and rendered the traverses along them highly interesting.' When they reached these, Fundi, his companion, baulked and refused to go further. 'I promised to follow you anywhere,' lamented the loyal Zanzibari, 'but how can I, when the path stands up on end?' The two had clambered north, either from Nyambeni West or Thego Valley, over Hohnel Valley and then into Teleki Valley.

But Gregory found the camp at the agglomerate too far from the central peak and glaciers to be of any practical use and, with Fundi and a young porter named Yussuf, moved to Teleki Valley where they camped under the shelter of some giant groundsel, 'near some old glacial moraines which ran across the valley like railway embankments'.

It was on his first excursion from this camp, at little under 15,000 feet, that Gregory became the first recorded victim of Mount Kenya's notorious and endemic altitude sickness which can be fatal. 'I was surprised and disappointed. I did not like to confess this to Fundi, as it seemed safer to keep him in absolute ignorance of the existence of this malady. . . . The attack was very slight, I soon recovered, and suffered no more inconvenience, except undue fatigue.'

Gregory wanted to study the glaciers, the Lewis Glacier in particular, but Fundi refused to wear the boots that Gregory had provided and the geologist sadly reconciled himself 'to the knowledge that whatever snow-work was necessary would have to be done alone'.

Before this work could begin, however, the trio had to endure one of the mountain's frequent hurricane-force storms, the fury of the wind bringing down a minor avalanche that wrecked their camp. Without light, 'there was nothing for it but to jump about, wrapped up in our blankets, to keep ourselves alive until the morning. The two Zanzibari suffered terribly, which, as the thermometer marked 28° [Fahrenheit] below freezing, was not surprising'.

As a result, the start of Gregory's climb to the glacier next morning — breakfast was impossible, their food was buried in the snowdrift — was delayed until some time after sunup but he was soon well ahead of Fundi and so rested on a platform at the snout of the glacier for his companion to catch up. 'That morning he was weak and ill, but he plodded steadily, though painfully, upward.'

A warm and friendly man, Gregory had reason for waiting. The loyal Zanzibari, who had also accompanied the Teleki expedition, 'had often talked to me about the great white fields he had seen with Dachi-tumbo (Teleki) and how disappointed he had been at not reaching them,' wrote Gregory. 'He had taken a keen personal interest in this expedition, and his influence with the men had been most useful.'

Now the geologist waited for Fundi to pass him so 'that he might be the first man to set foot on the glaciers of Kenya'.

Instead, somewhat to Gregory's surprise, Fundi climbed on to a boulder and recited the devout prayers of a Muslim. 'I could not,' records Gregory, 'understand all he said but sufficient to know that he thanked Allah for having enabled him to come where neither native nor white man had ever been before, and to stand on the edge of the great white fields he had seen with Dachi-tumbo from afar. He assured Allah that he was now more anxious to return in safety to the coast than he had ever been before, so that he might tell his friends of the wonders he had seen.'

When the prayer was finished Gregory invited the Zanzibari to step on to the glacier. But Fundi did not advance too far nor linger long. 'He went a few steps farther, and then, with a pleading look, said, "No farther, master; it is too white".'

Lighting a fire, Gregory boiled his thermometers and discovered that they were at an altitude of 15,580 feet. He prepared to go on upward but Fundi begged to go down. Since it was obvious that he was suffering from the effects of the altitude — more severely than Gregory's own attack — the surveyor, in fairness, released him to return to their camp.

Nonetheless, before Fundi left, the exhilarated explorer performed his own version of a Maasai war dance on the glistening ice of the great glacier and then began hurling snowballs at his astonished companion. If William Desborough Cooley had been the target it would have been bitter-sweet justice.

Gregory then went on alone, reaching a height that he estimated at 16,600 feet before being turned back by another ferocious storm. This would have placed him 300 feet or so above Point Lenana. He also over-estimated the height of Batian and Nelion by some 2,000 feet — and clung stubbornly to that belief as late as 1921.

'I stayed for a few minutes to pile some of the blocks of coarse rhyolite that occur there into a small stone man, under which I left a note of the date of the ascent,' he writes, 'and then ran down the Lewis glacier moraine to camp. . . .'

Try as he would, Gregory was unable to reach his elusive goal — the base of the central peak. The following day he was foiled yet again by the weather, after climbing over the northern ridge of Teleki Valley to Two Tarn Col, as he negotiated a traverse across Point Piggott. He could not see Batian or Nelion and was unable to take the single bearing that he needed to determine their exact positions.

His last glimpse was brief: just before sundown a rift appeared in the clouds that had lain over the mountain all day to expose the twin peaks for a few seconds. He never saw them again 'though I was . . . within range of view of the mountain for a month afterwards'. Finally, he had to retreat. Mount Kenya remained inviolate. But the glory of that last vision remained with him for the rest of his life.

'At my feet, in a deep valley, lay the snow-covered and crevassed Tyndall Glacier, beyond which rose the steep western face of the final peak. Unlike the eastern side this was almost entirely covered by snow and ice, and on it rested two small corrie glaciers (the Heim and Forel) supported upon ledges, the larger of them ending in a cliff of ice from two to three hundred feet in height. Huge masses frequently break off from the ends of both of these, and fall with a crash on to the margin of the Tyndall Glacier below, where they accumulate as fan-shaped piles of ice.

'To the north rose the steep pyramidal peak of Point Piggott, separated by a depression from the western aréte of the mountain. This ridge ends to the south as a cliff, which forms the northern boundary of the basin of the Tyndall Glacier. Couloirs of snow occur in places along it, and one at least of these might be practicable for a full-sized party, but a yawning bergschrund separated the glacier from the névé fields at the foot of the cliff.'

When he reached his camp in Teleki Valley, fully intending to return up the mountain, he found a note summoning him down to the base camp in the bog. The men, it said, were sick. He went, only to find to his consternation that the camp had been struck. Omari, acting on orders given in a letter in Gregory's name, forged by his cook, had retreated down into the forests. So ended the second assault on Mount Kenya.

But whatever Gregory's 'failures', in carrying out the first full scientific survey of this then virtually unknown mountain he performed supremely well. Utterly alone, he had explored unknown glaciers virtually on the Equator that had never been trodden by human feet, and ascended single-handed some formidable and daunting peaks. Moreover, his investigations gave the final answer to the doubting Thomases who had sneered at the reports of Johann Krapf.

Among others things, he proved that the peaks, in fact, were composed of plutonic rock, as Thomson had deduced from so far a distance; and were not, as Teleki had asserted from so close a distance, the remnants of a crater rim. Gregory is remembered today by the glacier, streaming down the north-east face of Batian, that bears his name.

But even the best can err. The mountain's height still remained a secret. Meticulous though he was, Gregory over-estimated its size considerably, affirming by his survey that it was at least 19,000 feet. He thought the highest point that he reached on Point Piggott was 'probably about 17,200 feet' (the actual height of its summit is 16,263 feet).

In a letter which was read in London, after a Royal Geographical Society lecture on Mount Kenya by Halford Mackinder on 22 January, 1900, Gregory argued with Mackinder's assessment and that of a survey by Captain Smith, both of which placed Batian at 17,200 feet, close to its actual height.

Undoubtedly, however, it was Gregory's book, *The Great Rift Valley*, published by John Murray of London, in 1896, that inspired Mackinder, who was later knighted, to attempt to conquer this giant on the Equator. Mackinder, studying geography at Oxford University, was fascinated by Gregory's exploits and his descriptions of East African flora and landscapes. He went to several of the geologist's lectures. The year that the book appeared, however, another explorer, George Kolb, attacking from the east, somewhere between Meru and Chogoria, attempted to reach the peak area and in fact penetrated to the high moorlands.

The heights of Kilimanjaro, 19,340 feet, were first scaled by the German Dr. Hans Meyer and an Austrian, Ludwig Purtscheller, on 5 October, 1889, two years after Meyer and his companion, von Eberstein, had been forced to turn back from 18,400 feet. And according to a suggestion in an unsigned report in the *Scottish Geographical Magazine* ten years after Mackinder's expedition, the news that a team of Germans were also planning to mount an assault on Kenya gave impetus to Mackinder's plans.

Mackinder set his sights on Kenya as much for the nature of its geography and that of the surrounding areas as for the challenge of climbing it, for he felt that in the Victorian era few people would have time for a geographer who was not also an explorer and adventurer.

'It appeared therefore that when the Uganda Railway had reduced the distance from the coast to Kenya by two-thirds, it should be possible, with no great expenditure of time, to convey a well-equipped expedition in a state of European health to the foot of the mountain, and such an expedition would have a reasonable chance of completing the revelation of its alpine secrets.'

Thus, three years after Gregory's book appeared, Mackinder left London with five companions, landing in Kenya only weeks after the railhead on the 'Lunatic Express' — the 1,000-kilometre-long railway between Mombasa and Lake Victoria — reached Nairobi.

Above: Sunlight perfects the ethereal beauty of a subspecies of giant lobelia above 15,000 feet. Named after Count Teleki, the first known European to reach the snow line on Mount Kenya, the subspecies occurs elsewhere only in the Aberdares and on Mount Elgon, which lies on Kenya's border with Uganda.

bove: Pastel pink flowers of an
pine thistle.

With photographer Campbell Hausberg as his second in command
(Hausberg also shared the expenses jointly with Mackinder), a botanist, E. H.
Saunders, and a taxidermist, C. F. Camburn, Mackinder also included in the
party two Italian alpine guides from Courmayeur, César Ollier and Joseph
Brocherel.

The aristocratic Englishman — he was later called the father of modern
geography — retained a vivid memory of the two Italians. In a 1930 tribute to
Ollier in the *Geographical Journal*, shortly after the guide's death, Mackinder
recalled their 1899 journey through the Suez, down the Red Sea, and up to
Nairobi from Mombasa.

'. . . nothing seemed to astonish them. They took everything as though they
had seen it before. We arrived on the Athi Plains just when the construction
camp at Rail Head . . . had moved on to the brink of the Kikuyu escarpment.
Except for the track of twin rails, pegged down on widely spaced sleepers, the
only signs of humanity in the broad landscape where now stands the city of
Nairobi were the green tents of three little camps — my own and those of the
District Officer and a trader.

'There one morning at dawn César and Joseph burst into my tent exclaiming
excitedly, "Monsieur, les montagnes!" I went out into the freshness of the
sunrise, and beyond great herds of game grazing peacefully within a few
hundred yards saw to the south on the horizon 100 miles [160 kilometres] away
the snowy dome of Kilimanjaro, and 100 miles [160 kilometres] to the north the
twin peaks of Kenya, streaked with glaciers. César remains imprinted on my
memory as he stood beside me at that glorious moment.'

In addition to the six Europeans, sixty-six Swahili porters from the Kenya
coast travelled upcountry to Nairobi by train. There Mackinder hired two
Maasai guides and ninety-six Kikuyu porters for the twenty-day march to the
central highlands.

It was not an ideal time for mountain climbing — or for travel through
central Kenya. Plague lay upon the land: smallpox had decimated the
Wakamba and the Maasai; and rinderpest had so thinned out the herds that
they were unable to lay in stores of meat.

During their march to the south-west base of the mountain the 170-strong
expedition was forced to live off the country at great risk. There was danger
from the hostile Kikuyu and the Maasai who were beginning to resent,
strongly, the European intrusion into their lands. At one stage, the Kikuyu
porters, cajoled by the 'dreaded Watumutumu' near Karatina, tried to desert
and were only checked by a display of firearms. 'Nonetheless,' reported
Mackinder, 'an arrow fell at my feet when we were traversing a thicket.' To
compound everything, the rains were exceptional.

By the middle of August the party had crossed the brawling waters of the
new-born Sagana and established their base camp high above the Laikipia. On
18 August, entering the forest close to the place where Gregory began his

Opposite: Early morning storm
clouds fret and boil over the
southern and western slopes of
Teleki Valley.

assault, Mackinder began what he expected to be a 'tedious passage of perhaps
three days'.

Mackinder now had good reason to bless his choice of the Italian guides,
woodsmen as well as icemen. These two cut through the bamboo to such effect it
took the party only one day to climb through the forest to the open moorlands.
'Hour after hour we forged onward, and after a time upward also, until with
unexpected progress we grew ambitious of making the passage of the forest-zone
in a single day. And this we accomplished with one hour to spare before the
inexorable tropical nightfall.

'We camped in a glade, part of the glade-maze which runs along the upper
edge of the forest, and above us, comparatively close was the green treeless
shoulder of the mountain, hiding the central peak.'

By the evening of the second day Mackinder had established his base camp on
the moorlands just above the 10,000 foot contour. By 21 August Mackinder and
the two Italians had begun their exploration of the upper reaches and discovered
for the first time the 'extraordinary vegetation of the alpine zone. . . .'

By careless chance they destroyed much of it for an extremely great distance
around their camp. A lighted match set fire to the heath. ' It never occurred to us
that where the ground was boggy to the tread any special precaution was needed
against fire.'

But within minutes the moorlands were ablaze.

'We had,' recorded Mackinder, 'created our own Krakatoa. Water was cupped
in the lobelia leaves and as the plants smouldered the water evaporated and
volumes of steam went up. This formed a great cloud of yellow smoke and white
moisture above us, visible at night time, as we afterwards heard, eighty miles
away. As the sun set, limpid greens and pinks coloured the sky high to the
zenith. The banks of cloud smoke were rimmed with orange and purple as the
sun changed from blood red to burnished gold. Afterwards the whole sky turned
a dull copper till it merged into the dense blackness of the velvety burnt hillsides.
In the midst of the blackened domes of grass the white silvery groundsel
gleamed out, and, rising high on three sides, was the red glare of the fire in the
neighbouring valleys. Behind us, towards the centre of the mountain, a space of
darkness testified that our combat had not been in vain.'

It was from this base that the porters were to carry supplies daily to a camp
Mackinder established next day in Teleki Valley at 13,870 feet. On the same day
Mackinder learnt that the porters he had sent to buy food from the local
communities at the foot of the mountain had been attacked and two were dead.

Thus, thirty-five porters, led by the two Maasai guides, were sent to Naivasha
to buy food. 'After going carefully through our stock we determined to divide
everything eatable between the men who still remained.' The rest were ordered
to follow the other party to Naivasha but they refused unless they were led by
one of the Europeans.

Mackinder decided to send the botanist Saunders with them, across the difficult and hostile valley between Kenya and the Aberdares and over that daunting mountain barrier — which reached well above 12,000 feet — to seek help and provisions from Captain E. T. Gorges, the government officer based in Naivasha, which lay at the western foot of the massif.

Mackinder then made his way back to the camp in Teleki Valley, arriving on 30 August 1899. Wasting no time in preliminary surveys, he decided to attack the mountain at once. With the two guides he set out to attack the ice-couloir on the south-east face of Nelion, the secondary peak, crossing to the left side of the face and by late afternoon gaining the southern aréte well above 16,000 feet. (This route was first climbed by Phil Snyder in 1974 to mark the seventy-fifth anniversary of Mackinder's expedition. He named it 'Ollie's Folly'.)

But they were delayed by the difficulty of the climbing and night found them on the South-East ridge, 600 feet below the summit of Nelion. The three bivouacked on a foot-wide ledge, so narrow that they spent the twelve-hour-long night fighting sleep lest they fall into the abyss. At first light they began to climb the aréte but were turned back by an impassable chasm less than 350 feet from Nelion's summit.

The following day Mackinder rested as Hausberg set out with the guides on a circular tour around the base of the peaks looking for the easiest and most certain way to the summit of Batian. They did not find one. Even today, Mount Kenya remains a formidable challenge to the most skilled mountaineer; conversely, on some routes a stout walker can make it to the top of Kilimanjaro.

The three did reach the summit of Kenya's third-highest peak, 16,355-foot-high Point Lenana, but could see no easy way up the two main peaks.

The next day the two Italians attacked Batian via the clinging Darwin Glacier, a time-consuming and perilous approach requiring exhausting step-cutting but, overwhelmed by a fierce blizzard, they were forced to retreat over the south ridge of Nelion.

Mackinder was on the verge of abandoning the attempt in his concern about the fate of the party sent to Naivasha when Saunders returned with fresh supplies. Now, instead of retreating, Mackinder planned a final challenge on this virgin mountain astride the Equator. Since one bid by rock, and two by ice, had failed he decided to attempt a route combining both hazards. His diary tells the story:

September 12.

'The five porters are sent down, and César, Joseph and I are left. It is five weeks since we left Nairobi with 170 porters, and we seem strangely alone.

'We left camp for our final attempt at noon. At one o'clock we were halfway up the terminal moraine of the Lewis Glacier. There were many dead and some living tree groundsel on the lower edge of the moraine. At two o'clock we were on the south lateral moraine beside the crevassed and falling part of the glacier. There was a light wind blowing up the valley, and it was hailing.

'We continued by the south lateral moraine for an hour and then crossed the

Lewis Glacier to the couloir at its north-west head. The surface was covered with crisp new snow. We ascended the snow in the couloir for a little, and so gained the top of the talus [scree] which lies at the foot of the eastern face of the great south aréte. The cloud had gradually risen from the glacier and we could see our track across the white expanse. There was still an occasional hailstone. . . .

'By 5.30 we had climbed almost to the top of the aréte and were pitching our little Mummery tent on our ice axes in a very convenient niche high above the Lewis Glacier. At 6 o'clock the Equatorial sun set, but the air did not clear until the unusually late hour of 7 pm. We warmed a small tin of soup. The night was calm but our bed on the rock was damp and very hard. We had just room under our little shelter to lie side by side, and grew stiff and cold-footed.'

September 13.

'Up at dawn — 5.30 am — the sky was clear above, but below, to east and south, was the far-spreading sheet of the cloud roof over the plains, with a dark gulf beyond, probably the Tana Valley. The eastern horizon was lost in a mist of indescribably magnificent purples and reds, a vast abyss of mere colour. We were away upward just as the sun showed over the horizon, giving us a grateful touch of warmth. Soon we reached the site of our previous bivouac on the crest of the aréte [the south-east ridge of Nelion]. Then we descended on to the ice-slope [the upper Darwin Glacier] beyond, traversing by steps the top of the Darwin Glacier. Here a biscuit-tin marked the turning-point of the reconnaissance made two days before by César and Joseph.

'We now followed the aréte upward, thinking that it would guide us to the lesser of the two summits, and from this we hoped to cross by the col to the greater. But after half an hour it became too steep to climb, and we were obliged to drop on to the hanging glacier to our left which depended from the col between the summits. To cut steps across this glacier direct to the higher summit was the only way left to us. . . .'

It was 8.30 am, and the clouds were forming dramatic patterns in the sky around and above them but, as they paused before beginning to cut their way across, the peak was still clear.

Ollier and Brocherel, unaware of the contrary snow-and-ice conditions on Mount Kenya, thought cutting the steps was a matter of some twenty minutes or so. But Gregory had already discovered that though Mount Kenya snow was softer than that of the Alps, conversely the ice was harder. In the event, it took more than three hours to traverse 100 feet of ice. In tribute, Mackinder christened this appalling stretch of ice the Diamond Glacier. There could be no better name for the adamantine-hard ice glistens and scintillates like a jewel in the bosom of the twin peaks.

Mackinder's diary takes up the story again.

'At first we traversed the ice obliquely upward, each step requiring thirty blows with the axe. There was a thin covering of snow. Then we turned a little towards the base of the lesser summit, but seeing no foothold on the rock we resumed our oblique traverse upward towards the greater. The glacier was steep, so that our shoulders were close to it. Had we fallen we should have gone over an ice-cliff on to the Darwin Glacier several hundred feet below.'

Once across, they were on rock and within an hour or so, as the sun reached its noon zenith over the Equator, the three stood in triumph on top of Africa's second-highest point. 'A small platform a few feet lower adjoined the south-east corner of the crag,' recorded Mackinder, 'and from this I got two shots with my Kodak of the summit with César and Joseph upon it.'

It was not until 10.20 pm, hungry and weary, but triumphant, that the three arrived back in their camp.

'Our times indicate a slow descent,' recalled Mackinder, 'and I was the chief cause of this. Beyond a spoonful of soup at night-time, I had had nothing to eat for nearly thirty-six hours, except a few meat lozenges and an occasional bite of Kola biscuit. Starvation seemed the only remedy for the lassitude I experienced in our first attempt. The remedy succeeded admirably during the ascent but naturally had to be paid for during the later hours.'

Mackinder also recalled the glory of the light that evening and sitting later by the camp fire. 'Our thoughts and our words were divided between our conquest and the red cinders which spoke of home, until presently the scene around broke silently into our dreams, compelling worship. Then, as the fire dulled and our feet grew chilly the bark of a leopard ranging the hillside opposite reminded us of the early rise on the morrow, and with a drink of cold water from our camp spring we rolled ourselves up in our blankets without undressing, for warmth could not be wasted. . . .'

It was a hard-earned victory; and, in that era, not only an immensely brave achievement but an astonishing feat of mountaineering demanding extraordinary skills and stamina.

But Mount Kenya did not take such trespass lightly. Inviolate for millions of years, *Kirinyaga* remained unbowed. Another thirty years were to pass before another human being trespassed on that sacred peak, home of *Ngai*, God of the Kikuyu and the Maasai.

Opposite: Point Lenana, Mount Kenya's third-highest peak at 16,355 feet. Just to the left of the summit stands the metal cross of Pope Pius XI that was set in place by Catholic fathers from the Consolata Mission in Nyeri on 31 January 1933.

# 3 No Picnics on Mount Kenya

Imaginations were stirred by the conquest of Africa's second highest mountain. By British standards these were truly awesome peaks. Mount Kenya's combination of rock and ice, in particular, and the fact that only the most highly-skilled high-altitude climbers could hope to stand atop its summit, gave it proportions, at the turn of the century, that seemed to rival the challenges of the Himalaya.

To those who suffer from vertigo and other neuroses, the passion for climbing is inexplicable but among the major delights must be the views. To stand at these heights and survey the cloud-wreathed panorama of fluted ice walls, glaciers, hanging ice-cliffs, sheer rock walls, and the almost sheer scree approaches, the dangers faced, the hazards overcome, must surely be triumph indeed.

A risk which the trekker shares with the climber is that of mountain sickness: a combination of nausea, sleeplessness, headaches, and potentially lethal oedemas, both cerebral and pulmonary. Sudden ascents to heights of 12,000 feet and more, without acclimatization, lead to accumulations of water on the lungs or brain. Swift descent and prompt medical treatment is the only answer.

For those who do not fall to this malady, trekking and climbing can still be a tortuous affair, each step an exercise in foot-dragging exhaustion. At your side, a sheer drop of several hundred feet. In your head, a splitting pain. In your stomach, nausea. On your feet, blisters. In your eyes, water. 'Lie down, lie down', your body commands. But no. This is the Abode of God, not to be seen faintly, from a distance. Draw near and be mesmerised. Thousands yearn to climb it, many have died in the striving.

From almost any angle, the final line on both Batian and Nelion is a vertical pinnacle of rock. In a direct line — divided by a narrow ridge that dips down about 200 feet — the two peaks themselves are only about 500 feet apart and the difference in height between Batian and Nelion is only thirty-six feet. The centrepoint is saddled by the permanent thirty-foot-wide ice-crest of the Diamond Glacier. Poetically, Mackinder called this the 'Gate of the Mists'. For some reason he believed the mountain's name, Kenya, was a corruption of the Maasai word for mists.

Whatever his reasons, there could be no more apt name for this col where, almost every day of the year, the first faint wisps of moisture form fingers of mist to take a slender grasp on the sacred peaks and then consolidate their hold until the whole of the summit is covered.

Though it's easy enough, at ground level 11,000 to 12,000 feet below the peaks, to scorn the thought of the supernatural, few who stand at the feet of the holy spires of Batian and Nelion, or climb their heights, would deny the sense of reverence and awe they inspire; or the subconscious awareness of a spiritual presence that suddenly assails the mind.

Occasionally, the phantoms of drifting and billowing cloud part briefly and shafts of liquescent light bathe the spires and their smaller cohorts with an ethereal golden glow.

Previous pages: Imposing ridge on the final stages of the Mount Kenya ascent where unpredictable weather poses an additional challenge for climbers.

Above: Colourful Chuka Lancers have become a major tourist attraction. The Chuka farm the eastern slopes and are closely related to the Meru.

If Teleki, and then Gregory, had enjoyed the privilege of success in naming the outstanding features of Mount Kenya which they discovered, they left the supreme accolade to Halford Mackinder.

As the first to conquer the mountain it fell to him to name its major peaks. It was something that he had discussed beforehand at the Nairobi railhead with S. L. Hinde, the British administrator of Maasailand, and history can be thankful that both were men of perception and sensitivity. Fittingly, Hinde had suggested that Mackinder should make his choice from a selection of Maasai names.

'When I was out there,' recalled Mackinder, 'the great plains, which are now covered with farms, were of course vacant. . . . The Maasai then wandered over these plains, and were still to a large extent master of the region that had been theirs . . . but it was already evident that they were doomed because the white man was coming, and would want those great prairies for his farms. . . . The Maasai, although cruel, were a fine race.

'They thought of their god as dwelling on the peaks of Kenya, and I felt it was right that a memorial of the noble savage should there go down in history. The hero chiefs of the Maasai two or three generations before the white man came were Batian and Nelion, two brothers it was said.

'Lenana was the living chief of the Maasai at the time I was in East Africa. We took with us two Maasai, and they carried Lenana's knobkerry by way of a passport in case we met any Maasai out on the warpath.'

Thus he named the three highest points of God's Mountain after the Maasai's holy trinity of the nineteenth century: Batian, the seer and prophet who united the fractious Maasai clans into one hegemony for the first and only time in their history, and who predicted the coming of the European, the railway line, and the plagues which spelt the end of Maasai supremacy; Nelion his brother, and Lenana, Batian's son, the last supreme chief of the Maasai who, in 1904 and 1911, signed the pacts that surrendered their traditional grazing lands on the Laikipia, beneath the tribe's holy mountain, to the British.

Some three kilometres from these three peaks stand Mount Kenya's two other major peaks, 15,467-foot-high Tereri, and 15,433-foot-high Sendeyo, which Mackinder named after Lenana's older brother who lived until 1926.

But now he set about making the mountain's secondary features a lexicon of the history of the European in Kenya. Two glaciers on the lower, northern face of Batian he named after César and Joseph, his two guides; the valley beneath them after Campbell Hausberg, the expedition's photographer who, using a system known as the Ives process, took what were certainly the first colour pictures of Mount Kenya, and probably some of the first colour photographs ever taken anywhere.

Ironically, six years earlier Gregory had named the same valley in honour of Joseph Thomson; ironically because Hausberg had relied a great deal on the advice of John Thomson, the Royal Geographical Society's official photographer for whom Mackinder now named a minor crest beneath Nelion's southern face,

Point Thomson. So there is nothing to commemorate the Scotsman who vindicated Krapf.

The major valley running north-east off the mountain in the direction of Meru, Mackinder named the Hinde valley after the British administrator; and the sparkling sheet of water south-east of this, which spawns the Nithi River, he christened Lake Michaelson — after one of his closest friends. It lies beneath the sheer, 1,000-foot-high cliffs of Gorges Valley named after Captain (later Brigadier-General) Gorges who came to the expedition's rescue. On the other side of these sheer cliffs stands another, smaller sheet of water, Hall Tarn, which Mackinder named after Major Hall, the British officer who was in command of Fort Hall (now the thriving town of Murang'a).

Yet, to the early European administrators and settlers who flocked to Kenya in the first decade of the twentieth century, 'God's Mountain' remained a distant landmark. Rarely seen, and then only briefly at certain times of the year, it was left unchallenged even during the dry season.

Perhaps the early migrants to Kenya were too preoccupied with the challenges of carving out and taming the fallow land and fertile forests of what were now the 'white highlands', and turning them into productive farms, to set their eyes on climbing the sacred peaks. Indeed, from Mackinder's conquest several years of the new century elapsed before any others ventured up the mountain.

The first recorded twentieth-century visitors to *Kirinyaga*'s glaciers, Scotsman Macgregor Ross, Director of Public Works in British East Africa, and David Hutchins (who was later knighted), Chief Conservator of Forests, made an entire circuit of the mountain at around 12,000 feet — primarily to establish the scope and extent of its great forest belt. But they also climbed high above the western foot of the mountain to study four of the fifteen glaciers that then existed — three fewer than when Mackinder was on the mountain. Shortly afterwards, Kermit Roosevelt, son of Teddy Roosevelt, the former American President, launched an assault on the glaciers.

If it was the intention of any of them to attempt the summit they did not say so — nor did they do so.

Not long after these expeditions, Sandbach Baker, a British forestry officer, made a solo climb as far as the glaciers.

In March 1909 two missionaries, the Reverends Dr. J. W. Arthur, and A. R. Barlow, sent to establish a mission at Chogoria on the eastern slopes of Kenya, made their first attempt to scale the mountain. They did not get far. The view from the plains beneath had been too beguiling.

'The bulk of the mountain,' records Dr. Arthur, 'can be properly comprehended only by an attempt to scale it. Looking back now, with the experience gained, we see how little prepared we were for what is a very difficult piece of work.'

Despite the outbreak of the First World War in 1914, 'God's Mountain' continued to beckon Dr. Arthur. In February 1916, again with Barlow and a third missionary, the Reverend G. Dennis, they approached the peak from the eastern side. 'On the fifth day we made our final attempt to reach the summit, and reached Point Lenana — at 16,300 feet. We crossed the Lewis Glacier to the base of the main peak but failed to accomplish the remaining 1,000 feet of sheer cliff.'

Three years later, soon after the end of the war, the indefatigable missionary launched another attempt, this time accompanied by Jack Melhuish. They set out from Nyeri on 28 January, 1915, with seventeen porters carrying thirty-three loads brought up from Kikuyu, close to Nairobi. They had to cover twenty-two miles to the farm of the aristocrat Berkeley Cole whose land lay at the mountain's western bay — and they did it in a series of shuttles on a motor cycle with a sidecar.

This was to be the first really serious assault since Mackinder's, two decades earlier. First, the party attempted the West Ridge but had to abandon the attempt. They then decided to follow Mackinder's line to the summit and one morning, just after nine o'clock, crossed the Lewis Glacier with five barefoot porters, reaching the foot of the southern aréte within half an hour or so, just as the mist began to move over the summit.

'Leaving the boys there, Melhuish and I started off up the knife-edge of the aréte which proved by no means insurmountable. Its inner lip was overhanging towards the Darwin Glacier, but access was found on the Lewis Glacier side, and we were able to do a delightful bit of rock climbing [only to be] brought up by an impasse in the shape of a gendarme . . . probably the identical gendarme which had stuck Mr. Mackinder and his party in their first attempt to climb the peak. There was nothing for it but to descend.'

Arthur found that his bouts of mountain sickness did not help. As a qualified doctor, he was also fascinated to discover that neither his nor Melhuish's pulse rate increased very much no matter the altitude. 'There was another condition, however, which was extremely interesting and which I first began to notice in the expedition with Melhuish. I suddenly found, while resting on the southern aréte, that I was breathing in the peculiar manner known as "Cheyne Stokes", a condition that one finds normally only when a man is at his last gasp.

'I then discovered that Melhuish also had the same condition, and in the succeeding expeditions all the members were affected similarly in these higher heights. It did not prevent one from doing a considerable amount of work.'

Undaunted, Dr. Arthur went back to the mountain in February the following year with another missionary, the Reverend James Youngston, J. T. Oulton, and a man called Machin, but although the skies were clear, the cold and afternoon hailstorms thwarted them again at much the same height as Dr. Arthur had reached the year before.

The word defeat however was clearly not in Dr. Arthur's lexicon for within six months, this time with Sir Fowell Buxton, he tried yet again, this time from the southern base of the mountain. It took two days for them to cut their way through the primal forest and another three to reach the Lewis Glacier. And once again, at much the same height, 400 or 500 feet from the summit and tantalisingly close to success, the weather again turned against him. But his passion and that of his friends and climbing colleagues remained unabated.

Now the challenge of attempting to be the second team to stand on its summit was sustained in measure — by an inexorable tide that continued to sweep up the mountain but, at least for another decade, never over it. Notable among these alpine enthusiasts were Jack Melhuish, E. A. T. Dutton, Ernest Carr, and the Hook brothers of Nanyuki, Logan and Raymond. And although none attained the summit, their love of Mount Kenya extended all around, embracing the forests and the moorlands. They explored these, and the secondary peaks which stud them, to the full.

Remarkable for their endurance, perception, and character, these pioneers were also notable, perhaps, for a touch of eccentricity. Dutton wrote *Kenya Mountain*, a fascinating and unpretentious account of his 'failures' that was so successful it reprinted within a year, and Carr took his model-T Ford up the long track, which he cut at his own expense from the Chogoria mission to a moorland roadhead at about 14,000 feet — even now, the highest in Africa — just below the start of the climb to Point Lenana.

This fired imaginations in people who had never trespassed so high. Galton Fenzi, the colourful secretary of the Royal East African Automobile Association,

Above: Kikuyu warrior. Mount Kenya is the sacred mountain of the Kikuyu, who call it Kirinyaga. They believe it is the abode of Ngai, Creator of the Universe, the one God who bestowed the land around the mountain's slopes to the tribe.

was so enthralled by the idea that in 1921 he brought out a tourist brochure extolling the joys of 'Winter Sports on the Equator in Kenya Colony'.

Perhaps hiding a wry smile, Dr. Arthur pointed out that 'At an altitude of 15,800 feet and over, which is the snow sports' region on Kenya, exertion of any kind is a severe strain and only possible to those who are young and fit.'

Arthur and Carr were perhaps the most dedicated. Not only did Carr establish the Chogoria track, arguably the most beautiful approach, but with Arthur he also established the first two climbers' huts on the mountain, all at considerable personal cost. The Urumandi hut is at 10,000 feet and Top Hut is at 15,715 feet on the Lewis Glacier besides the frozen pool known as the Curling Pond.

The two huts were designed by Arthur and Melhuish and paid for by Carr and in January 1922, while launching his sixth attempt to reach the summit, Arthur, together with Melhuish and Carr, set out to install the huts. The wall sections weighed thirty-five kilos each and the floor sections seventy kilos. Simply lifting them up the mountain was a considerable feat — and erecting them something else.

Uncertain that such heavy loads could be carried up the Nithi River, they struck out on a completely unknown line — with the result that the sections for the Top Hut were left scattered on the sides of the valleys in the wrong place. During the course of this exploration they came across the source of the Ruguti River, a tributary of the Tana, which is born in a steaming, boiling hot spring at 11,800 feet and Arthur thought that 'here there might be formed later a health camp'.

Abandoning any hope of erecting the hut on this expedition, the climbers made their base camp around the Curling Pond alongside the Lewis Glacier.

This tarn had been 'discovered' by Melhuish and Arthur in 1919 when the Scotsman, there and then, gave Melhuish his first and only lessons in the ancient Scottish sport of curling thus earning the tarn its curious name. On this occasion, the climbers had carried skates with them.

Next morning, which was fine, the party skated for some while — at an altitude of around 16,000 feet, gliding and waltzing among the clouds that drifted over the glacier to the delight of the African members of the party, frequently amazed, and no doubt amused, at the often curious behaviour of the white men, *wazungu*.

Once again, Arthur's bid to become the fourth person to stand on top of Batian, or the first to conquer Nelion, was foiled by the unexpected and early onslaught of the wet season — after they had again reached a point not far from the summit. Nonetheless, it was Dr. Arthur, appropriately, who named two of the mountain's main vantage points beneath the summit, Point Peter and Point John, after two of the apostles.

He was delighted by every new 'discovery' and vista and noted that one benefit of his most recent attempt was that it had added to the knowledge of Mount Kenya's eastern geography. In tracing the course of the Ruguti River, he discovered that the river that ran through the Hobley Valley was, in fact, the Thuci which cut the downstream boundary between the Embu and Chuka districts.

Indeed, as they wandered around the high contours enjoying many of the mountain's wonders, including its diamond-studded necklace of twenty lakes, all these early enthusiasts savoured the joy of discovery. One lake is named Hook Tarn after the famous and eccentric Hook brothers. Raymond Hook named two rarely seen tarns at the head of Hobley Valley the Enchanted Lakes; and another, above Mackinder Valley, Polishman's Tarn after a Pole who sought his advice on the best place from which to photograph the sacred peaks and who was delighted with Hook's suggestion.

Others, too, also enjoyed the privilege of naming many salient features, particularly Dutton and Melhuish. They dubbed two or three along the Hobley Valley Carr's Lakes and, in 1924, after his porters swore they saw a lion on its shores, Dutton christened another Simba Tarn.

In one of these magical secret valleys there's another lake, Kikami Tarn, so named because of the many hyraxes that live on its shores. Kikami is the Kikuyu name for the hyrax. Another indigenous name, Gitchini Tarn, given by Melhuish in honour of one of his porters, is no more. It was renamed the Hanging Tarn.

Both men are themselves remembered: in Point Melhuish, above the western edge of the Lewis Glacier; and Point Dutton, above the Joseph Glacier.

In 1926, he and Melhuish made yet another expedition to Mount Kenya with the intention of scaling Batian or Nelion and Dutton's subsequent book, *Kenya Mountain*, published in 1929 by Jonathan Cape, of London, with its lyrical descriptions of the landscape and flora and percipient observations of the porters who accompanied them, enriched with humour, remains one of the classics of mountain literature.

His description of Nairobi, wearing 'the very look of a mining camp', in February 1926 will strike a chord with many citizens of the 1990s. 'Parts of the town,' he wrote, 'were littered with refuse; the streets were cumbered with a jumble of architectural abuses, by buildings half up, by the skeletons of buildings burnt down; and the roads were execrable.'

Dutton felt that one day there might arise a citizen who would proclaim to the world his pride in Nairobi. 'It is possible,' he wrote with heavy irony. 'What is not?' But in the meanwhile Nairobi remained a 'slatternly creature, unfit to queen it over so lovely a country'.

It was for this very reason, to escape the heat, dust, and dirt of the city, that Dutton and Melhuish set off for Chogoria and Mount Kenya. That evening, after a long, hard drive along muddy roads, tyres fitted with chains, the two arrived to a warm welcome from their porters of former expeditions.

'It was already evening when we reached Mbogori's village, as near as may be 150 miles [240 kilometres] from Nairobi. . . . There were many old friends, and we had no sooner left our cars than they were crowded around us, laughing and

Right: Family picnic at Urumandi self-service tourist lodge which stands above Chogoria at 10,500 feet.

jostling and cheerfully reminding us of the last time we were here. . . .

'We were happy in meeting these old friends again. . . . We knew that for many days these men were to be our only companions, sole partners in our many small endeavours.'

The next day the expedition began the long climb through the forest and bamboo to the moorlands and 'after seven long hours of tranquil sleep' Dutton was awake early on the morning of the first camp, eager to experience the pale blush of early dawn from on high.

'I waited and I waited, and thought that surely here is the dawn. . . . At last, out of this dim and solitary loveliness, at last dawn came.' A description of its glories beggared him and he turned to Robert Louis Stevenson who 'once wrote of a sunrise which fits the African picture well enough'.

'Out of the East it welled and whitened; the darkness trembled into light; and the stars were extinguished like the street-lamps of a human city. The whiteness brightened into silver, the silver warmed into gold, the gold kindled into pure and living fire; and the face of the East was barred with elemental scarlet. The day drew in its first long breath, steady and chill; and for leagues around the woods sighed and shivered. And then, at one bound, the sun had floated up.'

As did Dutton, those who have experienced dawn and sunrise in the bosom of the Nithi Valley on the slopes of Mount Kenya above Chogoria will testify to the timeless truth of Stevenson's prose.

Though there was abundant wildlife on the mountain, particularly elephant in

Opposite: Despite their rugged majesty the rocky minions of 15,467-foot Terere and 15,434-foot Sendeyo defer in size and grandeur to Mount Kenya's main peaks.

the forests, the party saw none and cleared the last of the elephant trails at around 10,000 feet. But then they came across the astonishing sight of a thatched village on the bleak and empty moorlands. Dutton discovered they were Kimeru farmers who had moved up the mountain to avoid the tax collector, much as the English used the tax havens of Guernsey and Jersey in the Channel Islands.

He was fascinated watching the porters kindle a blaze with firesticks after damp rendered the party's matches useless.

All were delighted to find the hut that had been scattered two years earlier across the moorlands in place by the Curling Pond where Melhuish gave another exhibition of skating to the 'amazement and delight' of the porters.

'The snow and the glaciers were all very well, but here was something: a white man dancing with knives on his feet.'

It was during this expedition, to their surprise, that they met another of the mountain's veterans, Barlow, who was exploring the moorlands and whose arrival was 'out of all expectation in these wild and unfrequented parts'.

Dutton perceived a very strong faith in the porters who regarded themselves as trespassers on the mountain. 'They believe that *Ngai*, their god, lives on Kenya or, as they say, he walks on Kenya. They believe him to be unapproachable. They believe that he inflicts penalties on those who invade his sanctuary. . . . They believe that, as well as by *Ngai*, the mountain is inhabited by *ngomas*, evil spirits.'

Dutton found that none would mention the mountain's name while they were above the forests. 'The legend is that anyone who is guilty of saying the name on the mountain, is guilty of impiety and will incur the anger of *Ngai*; and the *Ngai* will cause a great storm to come, and thunder and lightning, and will kill the impious one and those who are with him.'

Dutton must have felt something of the mountain's brooding presence for he was not inclined to scoff at these beliefs. 'It is often impossible to explain away the manifestations of these spirits, of *Ngai* and of the *ngomas*: men and women do die; children do fall into fits; and cattle do fall sick in the most unaccountable way.'

Again, Dutton's attempt on the peak failed. They had hauled a large ladder with them in the hope of crossing a deep abyss between two ridges which 'soon became an irksome burden, and we came near to abandoning it by the way . . . we managed, by pushing and pulling, by cursing and coaxing, to get the ladder up the perilously narrow route.'

It was all to no avail. 'The crumbling rock made our progress the slower, and as we got higher and higher we began to move with the caution of faint-heartedness. Yet in the end we arrived at the gap with one rung in the ladder smashed, and ourselves still strong and undaunted. And here our hopes were quite dashed, and all our labour ill-spent.'

The gap was more than twenty feet wide and 100 feet deep. Abandoning the ladder, which still remains on the southern ridge of Nelion, the party retraced its steps to begin the search for another route.

On a subsequent visit, twenty-two months later in December 1927, when Melhuish was away in England, Dutton escorted Thomas Scott-Ellis, Lord Howard de Walden, up the mountain.

It was on this expedition that Dutton and his friend hiked northwards towards Mugi Hill, the eroded, remnant rim of a parasitical crater, to explore the largest sheet of water on the mountain and Dutton exercised his proprietorial pride in Mount Kenya by naming it Lake Ellis in honour of his visitor.

'I might, with a twofold propriety, have named it Walden Pond; there cannot be more than a few square yards of difference in size, and the name is pat. But, when Thoreau dwelt on its shores, Walden Pond was fringed with oaks and pines, birches and alders and aspens, and willows and maples; and it went down to a depth of more than 100 feet, whereas I doubt whether our mountain lake could lay claim to a third of that. As for the trees, the only tree in sight was a giant groundsel which overhung the northern shore.'

Thus it was to be Lake Ellis.

The naming of the mountain's principal features, however, sometimes led to confusion and red faces. For instance, in 1936, one lake which had been discovered in the Hausberg Valley was named after the Duchess of Gloucester who had visited Kenya in the 1930s. The Duchess, 'greatly touched' by the Mountain Club of East Africa's kind thought, had 'much pleasure in giving her approval' via Captain Howard Kerr, a Buckingham Palace equerry.

There was just one small problem that the Mountain Club had overlooked. There was no permanent tarn in the Hausberg Valley — nor had there ever been. When this was brought to the committee's attention they were dumbfounded. In those days the club would never have lived it down if it was revealed that Lake Alice was non-existent. Dutton was instructed by the committee to find a permanent Lake Alice.

More problems arose. In a letter of 24 March, 1937, Clarence Buxton, the District Commissioner in Narok, protested to H. O. Weller, the club secretary, about Gandar's Lake on the north-eastern slopes above Meru.

'I do not claim to have discovered it myself but from the accounts I have read of Mr. Gandar Dower's discovery it must be the same lake which I saw in January or February 1927 while climbing Ithanguni [a recent parasitical crater] from Meru. I noted that the lake was not marked on the map and reported this fact to the Provincial Commissioner, Nyeri. . . .

'If by any chance Mr. Gandar Dower refers to another lake I apologise. The one to which I refer was marked on the map which I forwarded with my report of the expedition.'

Weller, extremely worried about both problems, confided his fears to another committee member, P. Wyn Harris (later Sir), in a letter. 'What I am afraid of is that the lake Dutton may choose to identify as Lake Alice is the one already named as Lake Gandar! . . . the one about which Clarence Buxton has already made a protest. The location of these lakes should have been confirmed by men

Above: Vervet monkey with infant.

who have seen them not merely from the air.'

With a touch of what many would consider justifiable despair, he added: 'It would not matter if the Duchess of Gloucester was not involved. We must identify a Lake Alice!'

Nonetheless, in the event, the disputed lake became Lake Alice on 6 May, 1938 — perhaps not entirely to Buxton's, certainly not to Gandar Dower's, satisfaction — at a meeting of the sub-committee on 'names for mountain features' which was chaired by Wyn Harris. It was resolved: '. . . that the large lake to the north of and immediately beneath Ithanguni be named Lake Alice, after HRH Duchess of Gloucester; and that any other unnamed tarns shall remain nameless until such time as it is discovered whether there are any appropriate native names for them, or impersonal descriptive names are found for them.'

If Melhuish and Barlow had depended on the glaciers named after them to carry their memories into posterity they would now be forgotten. Both have melted and vanished.

But no member of the club could have begrudged the names that Dutton had earlier bestowed on one of the mountain lakes and a minor peak at the head of Teleki Valley. Harris Tarn honours Wyn Harris, a former colonial officer in Kenya, and Shipton's Peak, a former farm manager at Nyeri, two of the greatest names in mountaineering history, both of whom later very nearly conquered Everest, and whose skills, resourcefulness, and courage are indelibly inscribed on the pages of Himalayan climbing history.

Wyn Harris joined the colonial service in Kenya when he left Cambridge in the 1920s and by 1927 he had already made one unsuccessful assault on Batian.

Eric Shipton arrived in Kenya in October 1928 to work on a coffee farm in the Nyeri hills. 'My work was interesting and my surroundings agreeable,' he writes in his autobiography, *That Untravelled World*, 'but what delighted me most was my proximity to Mount Kenya; its base was only twenty miles [32 kilometres] away. I had not seen it on my journey from Nairobi, so the vision which greeted me as I came out of my bungalow at dawn the following day seemed all the more fantastic.

'The northern horizon was filled by a gigantic cone of misty purple, capped by a band of cloud. Over this, apparently floating above a still sleeping world of tropical colour, was a graceful spire of rock and ice, hard and clear against the light blue sky. The sun, not yet risen to my view, had already touched the peak, throwing ridge and corrie into sharp relief, sparkling here and there on a gem of ice.'

Shipton was consumed by the challenge this vision represented. Since Mackinder no one had succeeded in climbing Batian again and Nelion remained unconquered. 'Small wonder, then,' he adds, 'that I was enchanted by this lovely mountain.'

To really appreciate Mount Kenya's mystic moods and beauty, as well as the enormous challenge of climbing its main peaks, you must travel through the

Opposite: Porters on the hard climb out of Teleki Valley with the self-service Teleki Valley Lodge, at 14,200 feet, in the background.

bamboo and juniper forests to the moorlands above 11,000 feet. At this height the waxing and waning snows and glaciers above appear translucent; and, 3,000 feet higher, the ice-cliffs sparkle and twinkle like jewels. The facets on the sheer face of the Diamond Glacier, shaped by nature's own gemsmith, the cutting edges of the fierce winds, have been fashioned into a unique African jewel that reflects the light of the early morning sun. But these are diamonds that change their shape and texture with the daily melting and freezing of the snows.

With the sun in the southern hemisphere during the first half of the year, and in the northern hemisphere for the second half, Mount Kenya is possessed of a unique phenomenon. During the first six months of the year when the sun is directly on the southern face this is ideal for rock climbing. The northern face, excluded from direct sunlight, remains iced-up and offers ideal ice-climbing conditions. In the second half of the year, within days of the solstice changing, the position is reversed.

Watching the mountain each day, Shipton began to read its signs and its changing moods. 'For my first few weeks, until the short rains came, the mountain was generally clear in the early morning. Usually, too, the clouds would dissolve in the evening to reveal the peaks. The unveiling varied daily: sometimes the twin summits would appear above the cloud mass, looking incredibly high and remote; sometimes the glacier skirts would come first into view, grey and cold under the dark pall; sometimes a window would open to show a section of flying buttress and deep ice-filled couloir, steep and forbidding; sometimes the clouds would drift away from the west to reveal the peaks already golden in the sunset glow, shreds of rose-tinted mist clinging to their sides.

'In the brief tropical twilight the revelation was always fleeting. I never failed to watch it, entranced and exquisitely tantalised.' Shipton determined to attempt a conquest. 'Happily, by a wonderful stroke of fortune, I did not have to wait long for a chance to realise my dream.'

He wrote to Harris, who was an assistant District Commissioner in Kakamega, asking if they could join forces. Harris, who was nearing the end of his first tour of duty and preparing to leave for a holiday in Britain, suggested that if Shipton could join him at the end of December he would postpone his sailing date for three weeks.

Soon after this, Shipton fell off a cliff into the fork of a tree, breaking, unbeknown to him at that time, his ankle. 'Terrified lest this should ruin everything, I made as light of the injury as possible, though at first I could only hobble with a stick.' Then Shipton's dreams were dashed by a telegram from Wyn Harris cancelling his climb because of 'some disturbance in his district. I was desolated'.

Desperately, Shipton cast about for another companion with whom he could make the climb, suddenly remembering that Gustav Sommerfelt, an old friend, had come to Kenya to work on a farm near Eldoret. 'He had no climbing

experience, but I thought that together we would at least be able to make up a reconnaissance of the peak; so I wrote to him explaining the situation and imploring him to fill the breach. . . . His response was swift . . . and my spirits revived a little. Finally, on Christmas Eve, another telegram from Wyn saying that all was well sent them soaring as high as the peak.'

The three met in Nairobi on 31 December 1928 where they bought enough supplies for sixteen days and then set off in the early afternoon for Chogoria Mission at the eastern foot of the mountain in a hired lorry.

Their driver's fears of the elephants that infested the lower slopes of the thick forest never materialised and Wyn Harris noted wryly that 'the technique of avoiding elephant as a branch of mountaineering art has yet to be discovered'. They arrived at the first camp, deep in the forest, well after midnight. At dawn, they paid off the lorry and recruited fifteen Meru warriors as porters, Shipton impressed by their 'lithe, long-muscled bodies'.

Despite his broken ankle, he delighted in the contrasts he encountered on that first day's march to the moorlands and the 'delectable surroundings' of Ernest Carr's Urumandi Hut at 11,000 feet where Vivienne de Watteville, the Swiss author of *Speak to the Earth,* had installed herself in December for a two-month stay on the mountain. She had been unable to resist the description of Mount Kenya's charms by a friend in Nairobi which had filled her with 'a longing to be off . . . the urge of the mountains is the strongest of all'.

Miss de Watteville had already transformed the hut into a home from home, bookcases and bed covers, fernpots, and pictures on the wall.

Together the four celebrated New Year's Day. As they sat around the campfire that night, she was enthralled by their plans to climb the great peaks where, as she wrote, 'sky and earth brimmed over with rollicking blue; the very wind blowing off the snow sped down on wings of light; the hills danced and the heavens laughed for joy'.

On 2 January, 1929, well up on the moorlands, after passing Lake Michaelson and the dramatic falls that plunged hundreds of feet into the lake — which they later named Vivienne Falls in honour of Miss de Watteville — the three men had their first close views of the great peaks. They made their base camp at the head of a gorge at around 14,000 feet.

Next day they began their reconnaissance in earnest. 'Mackinder's ascent of Batian and all the subsequent attempts had been from the south-east, and this was the line of attack we had intended to follow. But our distant views of the north-east face of the peaks encouraged the hope that it might offer a practicable route.'

The next morning they moved their camp to the crest of a saddle just over a kilometre from the head of Mackinder Valley. The north-east face danced temptingly before them in the sun. 'We examined it carefully with binoculars, and though an ugly-looking bulge in the upper part of the face seemed likely to be very difficult, we thought it could be negotiated by one of several cracks.'

They went forward and climbed several hundred feet, delighted to find that the rock was as firm and clean-cut as Chamonix granite and that there was nothing to 'chasten their confidence'.

Unable to sleep from anticipation of the next day's climb, neither Shipton nor Wyn Harris had any doubts 'that, the very next day, the summit of Batian would be reached for the second time after a lapse of thirty years'.

In true alpine tradition, they had chosen the most direct route, one following most closely the line that water falling from the peak would take. But, not far beyond the point they had reached the previous day, the climbing became increasingly difficult, 'our progress, already hindered by the presence of a third man on the rope, became slower and slower'.

It was mid-afternoon. If they succeeded they would have little time to retreat before dawn. But within 400 feet of the actual summit their way was barred by a smooth, sheer eighty-foot-high wall, 'quite holdless except for a repulsive-looking crack'. The cracks by which they had hoped to climb the wall, in fact, were shallow rounded grooves 'offering little purchase and overhanging in their lower sections'. Thoroughly dejected, they retraced their steps reaching the base of the rocks just before sundown. The route, known as North Gate, remained unclimbed until 1980, when Iain Allen and Ian Howell pioneered this, the last great challenge left on Mount Kenya.

Next day they moved their camp around to the Curling Pond on the other side of the mountain and surveyed their new route, which followed in the footsteps of Mackinder, up to the crest of the south ridge of Nelion, 'narrow and serrated like a saw'. But their hopes were shattered again by a smooth pinnacle which they knew they could neither climb nor pass.

'There was blue sky above us, and it seemed for a while as if we were standing on a rocky islet in the midst of a storm-tossed sea. Then the towering buttresses of Batian and Nelion appeared; the rays of the setting sun broke through and, in the east, sharply defined, a great circle of rainbow colours framed our own silhouettes. It was the only perfect Brocken Spectre I have ever seen.'

Next day, when they set out in the gloom of early morning up the Lewis Glacier and crossed over to the base of Nelion's south-east face they were depressed. 'This now seemed to be our last hope,' writes Shipton, 'but in the cold, grey light it looked anything but promising.' By 8.30 am, after a gruelling climb during which they came upon an old rope belay used by Mackinder's party, 'white and threadbare with age', they reached the top of the south ridge where it joined the upper wall of Nelion and stopped to rest.

Warmed by the sun, their despondency vanished. 'We looked over a vast sea of cloud, a gently rising tide that would soon envelop us. To the south, a great dome of shining ice stood above the white billows. It looked so close that it was some moments before we realised that it was Kilimanjaro, nearly 250 miles [320 kilometres] away.'

Above: Black and white colobus monkeys haunt Mount Kenya's forests. Their survival is threatened by the destruction of their habitat.

Later, however, Shipton was filled with despair when he found 'a great overhang, which had been hidden from the ridge below but which now appeared to dominate the entire upper face of Nelion'. He shouted down to Wyn Harris saying he was returning but the colonial administrator insisted on coming up to join him. It was, he said, too late to try another route.

It was a fortuitous stubborness on Harris's part. They found a gully beneath the overhang which took them on to a buttress. 'As we reached it, I noticed that we were already above the lower part of the great overhang. Beyond the crest we had expected to be faced with a smooth vertical cliff: to our astonishment we found ourselves on easy, broken rock.

'We could not see the summit but it was obvious that we were already above the great eastern wall, and that there was now nothing to stop us. For the second time that day we experienced a dramatic reversal of fortune; this time, the certainty of success made it still more intoxicating. Only an easy scramble remained and we were there on the hitherto untrodden summit of Nelion.'

At forty-five minutes before noon on 6 January, 1929, they shook hands on top of 17,022-foot-high Nelion, the first men ever to do so; Shipton, be it remembered, with a broken ankle. He only discovered this months later, after an x-ray.

'Though by then the peak was wrapped in cloud, we could just discern the rocky dome of Batian, After a short rest we started down the ridge towards the "Gate of the Mists". Our first attempt to reach it failed, but by cutting steps down an icy slope above the north-east face, we turned an overhanging pinnacle and so gained the col. From there we climbed to the summit of Batian at 1.30. It was hard to believe that barely six days had elapsed since we left Nairobi.'

Both were greatly impressed by what they had achieved but 'standing on the summit . . . with the cold, damp mist swirling about . . . were far from confident that we could find the way down before dark. But we need not have worried, for every step of the route had been so engraved on our memories that we were never at a loss.' Tired and 'utterly happy', they reached the base of the peaks at sundown and made their way across the Lewis Glacier in the sunset glow.

Though neither of them wanted to do it, after some persuasion they repeated the climb two days later with Gustav Sommerfelt. In fact, freed from tension, they enjoyed this experience much more than their first climb. 'The weather was perfect,' remembers Wyn Harris who reported that Kilimanjaro was visible from Nelion.

When they returned down the mountain that evening they found that Miss de Watteville had set up camp next to theirs at the Curling Pond. 'She had seen us on the peak during the day,' recalls Wyn Harris, 'and very kindly crossed the glacier to meet us at the foot of the rocks with food and hot tea.' Next morning the three escorted her on a ramble around the base of the twin peaks.

Even though the weather broke that afternoon the three men, she reported in the *East African Standard* of 2 February 1929, remained in exuberant spirits.

'During the evening and night, hail driven by piercingly cold winds descended, but nothing could chill the spirits of the glorious three who laughed and sang till silenced by sleep.

'In the morning they went off in gusts of hail and wind and we were left in solitary possession of this polar spot.'

All this was part of a front page story in which Shipton and Sommerfelt also recounted their experiences. They wanted to recover some of the expenses of their expedition which had cost them £15 each. 'Wyn, who was drawing a princely salary of £30 a month, would have no part in this vulgar ostentation.'

Shipton had thought that their 'modest, factual account' illustrated by their pictures would make a discreet column inside the paper. But, in fact, it occupied most of the front page under the banner headline 'New Conquest of the Twin Peaks of Mount Kenya' — and the back page was filled with their pictures.

For this, the two shared the magnificent sum of £2 10s.

Meanwhile, up at the Curling Pond, Ernest Carr arrived with a large retinue of porters to lessen the author's solitude. 'The object of the expedition which was undertaken by the writer [Carr] and Mr. Desmond Moloney was to rebuild the hut at 16,000 feet by the frozen pond which was blown to bits by furious winds two years ago. . . . Our safari consisted of eighty boys to carry the material . . . two Indian carpenters, and a native cook. . . . The fundis crept out at 10 o'clock and commenced the work of re-erection and the way they stuck to their work in unpleasant and depressing circumstances is very praiseworthy. . . . Day by day the work progressed. . . .'

This cheerless aspect of Mount Kenya at its greyest and coldest did not deter Shipton. His trouble was that he had nobody to climb with. Wyn Harris had been posted to carry the British flag in the searing wastes around Lake Rudolf — 'so remote it was impossible to take local leave'.

But eleven months later, with Patrick Russell, a young Nairobi lawyer who had never climbed before, he completed his third ascent of Batian. He had planned to attack the West Ridge during this expedition but he was weakened by an attack of malaria. Nonetheless, he and Russell also completed the first ascent of Point John. Like a leaning tower of Pisa, its pyramid summit is dramatically aslant as it stands in the shadows at the base of the two major peaks.

When Shipton recovered, however, his thoughts turned again to conquering that tantalising western ridge. The problem was not how to do it but with whom. The answer came in a letter written by a farmer at Sotik who had read of his latest conquest in the *East African Standard* and wanted Shipton's advice on how to climb Mount Kenya. H. W. Tilman's letter was the beginning of one of the most famous partnerships in the history of men and mountains.

Shipton was impressed and invited Tilman to join him on an expedition to Kilimanjaro 'which, despite the fact that the mountain is little short of 20,000 feet high, is nothing but a long and, in the conditions we encountered, somewhat gruelling walk.' The two also climbed the much more severe and testing

Mawenzi, similar in height to Mount Kenya. It was all Shipton needed to know.

'I soon realised that my new companion (it was many years before I called him "Bill") . . . was ideally suited to the game. I asked him to join me six months later in an attempt to make a complete traverse of the twin peaks of Mount Kenya by climbing the western ridge of Batian and descending by our old route, a project I had cherished ever since I had first seen that glorious ridge.

'The West ridge is the most beautiful thing on the mountain, and though it is of tremendous length, the eye is irresistibly drawn thither from the impossibilities of the neighbouring faces. It has its origin in a col between Point Piggott and the Main Peak, and rises in a series of great sweeps to a point where it meets the north-east ridge; then it turns south and runs to the summit of Batian.'

The memory of that vision stayed with Shipton throughout his life. If the Himalaya were his supreme love, Mount Kenya was his first love. Despite the magnificence and assortment of mountains that he discovered later in the Himalaya, Kenya still held its place in his affections. Indeed, after all that he achieved, he was able to say in 1969, forty years after he first climbed Mount Kenya, that 'few mountains have such a superb array of ridges and faces.

'From the summit of Batian a sharp, serrated crest runs northward for some distance before dividing into two main ridges, one plunging steeply to the north-east, the other descending westward in a series of huge steps to a col dividing Batian from a massive peak known as Point Dutton.'

Aware of the futility of starting the assault from the Northey Glacier or of gaining it higher up the north face, the two had climbed Dutton Peak to survey the ridge from the best vantage point: a survey which was to prove critical to their eventual success.

When they did set out on 31 July, 1930, the ridge was all that Shipton had hoped. 'We were met by a really wonderful view of the West face. I think I have never seen anything so utterly appalling. Two glaciers are its chief feature and, with the exception of the summit rocks and a belt of ice-swept rocks below the upper hanging glacier, it offers the appearance of one vast ice wall.'

They had chosen this time for the climb because the face was clear of ice and they would be climbing on rock most of the way. During their survey, Shipton and Tilman singled out the col between Petit Gendarme and Point Piggott as the pad from which to launch their attack. They would move towards the gap behind Petit Gendarme by traversing from the south.

In total darkness, they set off from the Joseph Glacier but found the face in dreadful condition, snow and ice in various degrees of stability. As the sun rose, well-established pitches turned into a wall of treacherous slush, the very conditions they had hoped to avoid. Several times they thought of abandoning the attempt.

But they struggled on hoping to find better conditions when they reached the northern side. Eventually, just before noon, they found themselves across and over and instead of snow and ice they were on dry, warm rock. It was deceptive however: the rock was crumbling and unstable.

In all that they would experience later in their years in the Himalaya, on the slopes of the greatest of all mountains, Everest, and its scarcely less daunting cohorts, this was the one climb that tested Shipton and Tilman to the limits of their stamina, endurance, skills, and spirit.

'One after another pinnacles loomed into view, greatly magnified by the mist; one after the other we set about the problem presented by each new obstacle, always hoping that it would be the last. I lost count of time; the ridge seemed to go on for ever, but at least we were going with it; surely nothing could stop us now.'

It was a most daunting climb but twelve hours and some minutes after they set out they reached the summit, bathed in the glow of the late afternoon sun. 'At last, in place of the sharp spire we had come to expect, a huge dark-grey mass appeared before us and my last doubts vanished. A few steps cut into an icy gully, a breathless scramble up easy rock and we were standing beside the little cairn which I had helped to build on the summit of Batian.

'It was 4.30 pm. There was no chance of getting down before dark, but I was much too happy to be bothered about that. Needless to say, much of my joy stemmed from sheer relief, for . . . failure to reach the summit would have placed us in an ugly situation, and the situation had remained in doubt till the last few minutes. Bill had been magnificent; he had shown no sign of anxiety throughout the climb, and his stoicism no less than his innate skill in climbing and handling the rope made a vital contribution to our success. . . .'

Now came the long descent, following in grim conditions and darkness the route, via Nelion, thus traversing all the main peaks from north to south. For Shipton, who began to vomit, it was particularly exhausting and the two did not reach camp until twenty-four hours after they set out.

'The traverse of the twin peaks of Mount Kenya was probably the hardest climb I have ever done; though no doubt the cumulative difficulty was greatly exaggerated in my mind by the fact that the ascent of the west ridge was all over virgin ground.'

Within the next few months Shipton and Tilman laid claim to virtually the whole mountain. In the same season, during the dry period of July–August in 1930, they made the first climbs of Point Peter, Dutton Peak, Sendeyo, Point Piggott, and Midget Peak, in a partnership that became pre-eminent in the history of British mountaineering.

For when they had exhausted the potential and possibilities of 'God's Mountain', they turned their skills and ambitions to the mightiest peaks on earth — as sacred to the Hindus of Nepal and India as *Kirinyaga* to the Kikuyu. In 1931, Shipton who was then only twenty-three, reached the summit of 25,447-foot-high Kamet, above the Raikana Glacier of Tibet, with Frank Smythe.

Two years later, under Hugh Ruttledge, he and Wyn Harris were members of

Overleaf: Porters and climbers
negotiate steep slopes of scree
and rock on the approach to the
foot of the final pyramid of
Batian and Nelion where the
real climbing begins.

the British expedition which reached Everest after a six-week march over the Tibetan plateau. Selected to make the first bid for the summit, he and Smythe established a camp at 27,400 feet. Both felt the debilitating effects of altitude, Shipton more than his colleague. Altogether they spent a total of nineteen days above 23,000 feet. But their bid failed.

On 30 May, 1933, Wyn Harris and Wager set out from the same camp for the summit but were forced back. Shipton believed that his Mount Kenya companion would have made it if they had carried oxygen.

Tilman, something of a loner and not fond of large expeditions, was a taciturn man. In 1934 he joined Shipton in the Himalaya where they continued to speak to one another in monosyllabic terms always addressing each other as 'Shipton' and 'Tilman'.

'When, after another seven months continuously together, I suggested that it was time he called me "Eric" he became acutely embarrassed, hung his head and muttered, "It sounds so damned silly".'

They made a reconnaissance of the impenetrable walls surrounding the basin of 25,645-foot-high Nanda Devi with its peerless spire, 'ever changing in form and colour as we moved'.

The next year, the two put together an Everest survey party in anticipation of the next British expedition which, in fact, Shipton joined the following year. Tilman, who had problems acclimatizing to heights above 20,000 feet, was not chosen but nonetheless in 1935 he and Shipton indulged in a 'veritable orgy' of mountain climbing, reaching the summit of twenty-six peaks — all higher than 20,000 feet.

Tilman's exclusion turned out to be fortuitous for him. He was invited to join the 1936 Anglo-American expedition to Nanda Devi and, with Odell, he reached its summit in what is generally regarded as the greatest mountaineering achievement of the pre-war years. His susceptibility to mountain sickness was noticeably absent.

It was six years after Tilman's and Shipton's conquest of Kenya. The heights of Nanda Devi represented the highest peak on earth reached by any men and remained so until 1950 when Frenchman Maurice Herzog — the first to be given a permit to tackle the giants of Dhaulagiri and Annapurna — and his colleague Louis Lachenal crested the brow of Annapurna's north face on 3 March, 1950, and looked down from the 26,545-foot-high peak of the world's tenth-highest mountain.

Before 1950 most of Nepal's peaks were shrouded in mystery, virtually unknown except for those that could be reached from Tibet, the point from which all the early assaults on Everest were made. But when Nepal opened its doors to foreigners in 1950, much of the pioneering work, on which many climbers depend even today, was carried out by Eric Shipton and H. W. Tilman, as on Mount Kenya. They were the first climbers to venture into Nepal's hidden mountain sanctuaries.

One of Tilman's 'discoveries' was Langtang Himal and its many marvels — just seventy-five kilometres north of Kathmandu, it was unknown then, even to many Nepalese. With its monasteries, Buddhist *stupas*, prayer walls, and places made sacred by the Hindu scriptures, it is one of Nepal's most enchanted regions. As Tilman toiled through the upper reaches of the Langtang Valley, he was captivated by the size and beauty of its towering peaks and precipices. He called it 'one of the most beautiful valleys in the world': still considered an understatement by many.

Both men were in the 1951 Everest Expedition led by Shipton who at the last minute agreed to include climbers from the Alpine Club of New Zealand who were already in Nepal: Earle Riddiford and Edmund Hillary. Shipton, who was not sure that he had done the right thing, commented, 'My momentary caprice was to have far-reaching results.'

For it was Hillary, with the Sherpa Tensing Norgay, whom Shipton had first met as a nineteen-year-old newcomer to mountaineering in the 1931 Everest expedition, who finally conquered 29,028-foot-high Everest, the world's highest mountain, two years later. But Shipton, who had also been appointed leader of this expedition, was not with them. He had resigned in protest after a series of political moves to include John Hunt as co-leader.

Nonetheless, his name, and those of Wyn Harris and Tilman, remain etched as firmly on the history of the Himalaya as that of Mount Kenya. Shipton's and Tilman's ascent of Batian was only the fifth and though, during the 1930s and 1940s, many more were to try, few succeeded. Mount Kenya was ever a defiant mountain.

After Shipton and Tilman struck their last camp and headed off to the greater heights of Nepal and Tibet, Batian and Nelion continued to rule the mountain moorlands aloof.

Raymond Hook, Dutton, and others — among them a Kenya lawyer, Humphrey Slade who in the vanguard of Independence became the first Speaker of the new nation's elected Parliament — continued to pay homage at their feet but not to climb. They carried with them trout spawn and fingerlings to stock these highland streams and ice-cold tarns — a heritage that survives in the streams to delight fly fishermen in the 1990s. But although the fish flourished in the tarns they did not breed and gradually died out.

Nobody loved Mount Kenya more than Raymond Hook. The mountain, affirmed Slade, was Hook's 'first and final love'. After his death, Slade described him as Mount Kenya's unofficial warden, long before it was established as a national park in 1949. 'He explored almost every part of the Mountain from forest to glacier, made maps, named landmarks, blazed trails, stocked lakes and streams with trout and organised countless safaris for mountaineers, scientists, sportsmen and others.'

Those days in the 1930s must have been halcyon. With few visitors, the moorlands remained the lonely but privileged preserve of Hook and his friends.

'A safari with Raymond on Mount Kenya,' remembered Slade, 'was an unforgettable experience. The apparently casual preparation at his Nanyuki home, which nevertheless produced all that was needed, even for emergencies; the start of the march with pack ponies and mules, headed by this massive figure on his splendid stallion (Bronx); the disreputable but cheerful and competent company of henchmen, and miscellaneous dogs; his intimate knowledge of every beast, bird or flower that we met on the way; the adventures in forest, swamp, rocky places, mist and snow; and at the end of each day, the camp, in less and less comfort, when a soft voice came out of the darkness beyond the fire (if any), to talk about the martyrdom of man, the dreams of H. G. Wells, or his own belief that he had found on the Mountain traces of an extinct race and that he knew their ways.'

No doubt, these parties camped in one of the many amphitheatres that surround Mount Kenya's sacred peaks and form natural cathedrals. The reverence these inspire, even in the most cynical, is profound.

The Italian fathers at the Consolata Mission, Nyeri, felt this reverence so deeply that when Pope Pius XI sent the mission the gift of a cross they decided to place it near the summit of Mount Kenya.

On 31 January, 1933, they climbed the slopes of Point Lenana and set the cross firmly in place among some rocks just below its summit, symbol of the feelings which this sacred mountain had provoked within their hearts.

But Batian reigned supreme. Indeed, it was not until six years after Shipton's climbs with Tilman — indeed, as Tilman was climbing the slopes of Nanda Devi — that another person stood again on Batian's summit. This was H. J. Irens and his companion, E. Sladen, of Britain, who followed Shipton's trail-blazing route, now referred to as the Normal Route, to the top in 1936.

In 1937 an Italian, Piero Ghiglione, and a Swiss, Eduoard Wyss Dunant, were successful. Initially, they followed Shipton's route, before pioneering a new route up a section of the southern aréte of Nelion.

The following year, 1938, might well be described as Women's Year in Mount Kenya's history. In February 1938 a party reached the summit of Nelion: the fourth member, Miss Carol Carroll, was the first woman to stand on either of the peaks. Just a month later Batian, too, fell to the feminine touch of Miss Una Cameron, accompanied by two guides, Eduoard Bareux and Elise Croux, who like Mackinder's accomplices were also from Courmayeur.

Nothing tells us what kind of persons Miss Carroll and Miss Cameron were, but for women at that time to surmount the obstacles and high-altitude, treacherous glaciers, and sheer drops found on Mount Kenya, not only called for exceptional stamina, endurance, and courage but a touch of defiance towards the attitudes and mores of conventional society. It was formidable achievement.

Nor were they alone. On the very next day — 6 March 1938 — E. Sladen, who had returned for a second assault, scrambled up the last few feet of Batian to repeat his earlier success and give his companion, his sister Miss G. Sladen, the

Opposite: Sunrise over the
Hohnel Valley unveils many
magnificent features of Africa's
second-highest mountain. From
left: Western Terminal, Arthur's
Seat (with Midget Peak in
foreground), Point Piggott (with
Point John in foreground),
Batian (the major summit,
where Nelion shadows the Gate
of Mist and the Diamond and
Upper Darwin glaciers),
Thomson's Flake, Point
Thomson, the Lewis Glacier,
and Point Lenana.

distinction of being the second woman on the peak. Again, we are told nothing of Miss Sladen's appearance but clearly she too was an outstanding athlete with little concern for prevailing convention.

It was also around this time that Matu Mathara, who had accompanied Miss Carroll's group, organised an all-African team to challenge Batian. But whether it succeeded or not is not recorded. There is evidence, however, to indicate that Mathara, in fact, was the first African to reach the summit of Nelion; though whether on this expedition, or on one where he was employed as a guide, is unclear.

For the researcher, the mystery deepens with the discovery near Thomson's Point, by Rufus Klarwill, a member of the Mountain Club of East Africa, of the body of a member of the African expedition. When Klarwill first heard about the African expedition from Hook he felt that he 'was deliberately vague about it'. In the event, some time later, Klarwill 'found a very well preserved, desiccated, body of a native on the ridge leading up to the normal route, nearly covered with stones under which he had obviously been buried by his mates'.

This unknown climber, in an unmarked grave, may well have been the first victim of a mountain that is undeniably hostile (it was estimated in the 1970s to claim at least one life a year, either from the pulmonary and cerebral oedema that is endemic to Kirinyaga on a scale unequalled by any other mountain, or from falling).

Another African doomed to die on the mountain some years later was Ali Mucemi, a Kikuyu porter who reached the summit of Nelion with Lord Malcolm Douglas-Hamilton in February 1941. The RAF officer, with Squadron Leader Arthur de Salis, had long dreamed of climbing Mount Kenya and saw his leave as a 'heaven-sent opportunity' to fulfil his ambition. But when they reached the Top Hut de Salis fell victim to mountain sickness and the officer decided to make his attempt with Mucemi, whom he insisted on calling Ari (no doubt, that is how Ali pronounced it because of the Kikuyu proclivity to mix their Rs and Ls).

'Ari had already been on one or two expeditions to Nelion, and had actually climbed up the greater part of Nelion, although he had never been to the top before. He was reputed to be able to climb up anything.'

It was said, wrote Lord Malcolm, that there was not a tree that he could not climb until a neighbour asked him to retrieve the honey from one of his hives. 'Ari . . . admitted that after all he had been wrong . . . he had struck a tree he could not climb.'

That night however Mucemi sneaked out, climbed the tree and took the honey for himself.

Lord Malcolm liked Ari immensely — not just for his companionship and assistance — and with good reason for without Mucemi it is unlikely he would have been able to attempt the climb on which he had set his heart.

Mucemi's mountaineering techniques were, however, to say the least, unorthodox. When he led on certain pitches, he unroped himself and tied it to a

rock — leaving it for Lord Malcolm to use as 'a sort of railing'. Moreover, climbing a buttress near the summit he used the ice-axe to hook into crevices and haul himself up on it.

Nonetheless, on that February day in 1941, with Douglas-Hamilton, Ali Mucemi Kikuyu became one of the elite group of brave people to stand on top of Nelion. But after two hours of struggle in mist and snow to cross the Gate of Mists to Batian, Douglas-Hamilton called off the attempt and set about the descent.

Tragically, eight years after this, while accompanying an Italian expedition, Mucemi collapsed and died climbing Mackinder's Chimney on the south wall of Nelion. Dr. Bernadelli, who was with him, had already reached the top when he felt the rope suddenly tighten. Mucemi had been stricken by a heart attack. Gently lowering Mucemi's body back to the bottom of the pitch, his companions buried him at the foot of the climb.

Of all the attempts on Mount Kenya in the first half of this century, however, none were so dramatic in their scale and ambition, nor so poignant in their failure, as that mounted by thirty-three-year-old prisoner of war Felice Benuzzi and his two compatriots, Dr. Giovanni Balletto, thirty-eight, and Enzo Barsotti, from behind the barbed wire of a Nanyuki compound.

Taken prisoner in Ethiopia in 1940-41, Benuzzi was transferred to Kenya, first to spend a year in a POW camp at Eldoret and then to Nanyuki. 'The next morning, 13 May [1942],' he relates in *No Picnic on Mount Kenya,* 'I was shaken out of my sleep by Umberto: "Quick. Get up. Come and look at Mount Kenya."

'I emerged at last, stumbled a few steps in the mud and then I saw it: an ethereal mountain emerging from a tossing sea of clouds framed between two dark barracks — a massive blue-black tooth of sheer rock inlaid with azure glaciers, austere yet floating fairy-like on the near horizon. It was the first 17,000-foot peak I had ever seen.

'I stood gazing until the vision disappeared among the shifting cloud banks.

'For hours afterwards I remained spellbound.

'I had definitely fallen in love.'

It was the last he saw of it for a long time. Day after gloomy day the mountain remained hidden. To Benuzzi, worried for his family held in detention in Ethiopia, bored by confinement and miserable, that one brief vision of those sacred 'tantalising' peaks beckoned more and more.

Then the rains ended and as he turned the corner of his barrack one night he saw it again. 'The white glaciers gleamed with mysterious light and its superb summit towered against the sky.

'It was a challenge.

'A thought crossed my numbed mind like a flash.' He decided to break out of camp — not to seek freedom but to climb the mountain.

'The more I considered the idea of escape, the more I realised the magnitude of the task I had set myself. . . . How should we make the actual climb? Whom

should I ask to accompany me? How would we get out of the camp and in again?'

Apart from the enormous climbing challenge there were other uncountable hazards. Half a century ago the forests and the moorlands teemed with intractable and ferocious wildlife. Mount Kenya was haven particularly to buffalo, rhino, and elephant and there were many lion and leopard.

'A fuel party of prisoners in the nearby forest,' wrote Benuzzi, 'had been attacked by a troop of elephants on transfer, and a prisoner who had been rash enough to approach them in order to see some baby elephants had been caught up by a mother, smashed against a tree and killed on the spot.'

Already that year the *East African Standard* had reported an attack by a herd of buffalo on one expedition led by a major and in 1944, the year after Benuzzi's magnificent escapade, Hugh Copley reported a buffalo killing a lion in a titanic struggle on the moorlands.

Lieutenant Colonel C. H. Stockley, writing in the *East Africa Annual* of 1942-43 reported that: '. . . Of the largest beasts, buffalo go to 14,000 feet . . . while the rhino like lying up in the giant heather.' Camping on the moorland just above the treeline at 11,000 feet, Stockley added that a herd of twenty-five elephant had spent the afternoon feeding on the opposite slope of a valley in which they were camped and were still there in the morning 'standing in an open grassy hollow which was white with frost: an incongruous sight, for elephants and frost do not go together'.

The eventual breakout from their prison camp, the struggle through the forest to the moorlands above, and their desperate attempt to climb Batian make dramatic reading in Benuzzi's best-seller.

Two of the men, Benuzzi and Balletto, chose to make their attempt — at altogether the wrong time of the year — up the West Ridge, approaching via the northern face of the Petite Gendarme. They were rewarded by what Benuzzi describes as 'one of the most amazing views of the whole trip' for a bank of mist covered everything below the 8,000 foot contour.

'On the undulating silver-grey sea of mist was cast the dome-shaped shadow of Mount Kenya surmounted by the tooth-like form of Batian, all in a dull brown-violet hue. The peculiarity of this natural shadow play was that from the very summit of Batian's image there rose a second shade-cone pointing to the west, together with an exactly similar, complementary light-cone pointing to the east. It was a phenomenon of reflection I am still not able to explain.'

By 11.00 am, the two were at the foot of the Gendarme, poised for the assault on the main peak of Batian. Fresh snow covered old ice making their progress snail-like. And, at 12.30 pm, 'rags of mist' began to creep down the north-west ridge as the wind grew stronger and stronger. Soon Balletto was lost above Benuzzi in the mists. They had reached a point on the final face that could well have been above 16,000 feet. Indeed, Benuzzi estimated that they were probably between 800 and 600 feet from the actual summit.

But ill-equipped and undernourished, the two had to retreat. Any attempt to climb further, Benuzzi comments, 'would have been unpardonable lunacy'. The retreat was infinitely longer and more difficult than their ascent but when they reached the point where their adventure had began, they paused.

'Before leaving for good the scene of our unsuccessful struggle we glanced back. Batian's north-west ridge looked grand, ice-sprinkled and partially enveloped in clouds.' With a true mountaineer's love of forbidding peaks, Benuzzi adds, 'Perhaps it looked even more superb for being left inviolate.'

Some time later, by some tarns at the foot of the Northey Glacier on their way to Point Lenana, the two rested awaiting daybreak. 'At last the sky between Sendeyo and Lenana blushed rosy. There was no breath of wind. . . . Always, and more especially on mountains, have I watched daybreak with deep awe. It is an age-old miracle which repeats itself again and again, every day the same and every day different. It is the hour of Genesis.'

And later, skirting the north-eastern face of Batian, where the pillars of rock supporting the cliffs look like gigantic organ pipes, 'Not by mere chance is the mountain climber induced to think of organ pipes or of altars as he looks up those towering rocks; it is a religious feeling which fills his heart. . . . the rock was covered by helichrysums clinging in a compact cushion and enjoying the sun. One could hardly believe that the flowers had grown there spontaneously; they seemed to have been put there, in homage to an invisible Madonna in a wayside shrine, by some wanderer who saw in the majesty of the mountain a sign of the Creator's might.'

Sometime after this they reached the summit of Lenana and hoisted the Italian flag, a symbol of their defiance — and pride. Within a week it was recovered by a party who saw it while scanning the mountain summits from Thomson Lake. 'If anyone wonders what it meant to us to see the flag of our country flying free in the sky after not having seen it so for two long years, and having seen for some time previous to this only white flags, masses of them, I can only say that it was a grand sight indeed.'

They left a note with their names sealed in a brandy bottle and descended.

Some days later the three returned to the prisoner of war camp as secretively as they had left — to be discovered during the following day's roll call. For their 'crime' they were sentenced to one month's imprisonment. But, full of admiration at their feat, the commanding officer released them from their cells after only seven days.

For the rest of this decade, Mount Kenya remained the preserve of Arthur Firmin, the final link in the quartet of incomparable climbers that dominated the mountain's history in the first half of this century — as three were to do in the second half.

Firmin, a Kenya-born European, was twenty-five when he returned to his homeland in 1937 after fifteen years of schooling and work in Britain where he became a photographer. He was put in charge of the Kenya Police photographic

Opposite: Western Terminal, near Arthur's Seat, one of the tough rock-climbing challenges beneath the main peaks.

section, but it was not until near the end of World War 11 that he was free to pursue his other passion — mountain climbing.

He was equal in his artistry and technical excellence to any of his predecessors. He had an uncanny ability to look at any mountain and visualise, as if by telepathy, the hazards and difficulties which had to be overcome.

Denied the privilege of being first or second on any of the twin peaks, Firmin nonetheless pioneered three of Mount Kenya's most classic climbs. With Peter Hicks, he completed the first ascent of the terrifying north face in July 1944; and with J. W. Howard the equally awesome first ascent of the south-west ridge in January 1946.

Finally, in February 1950, with J. S. Bagenal, he reached Batian via the Darwin and Diamond Glaciers.

Thus, in a few short years, he stamped his name upon Mount Kenya's history as indelibly as Shipton, Harris, and Tilman. It may well be that he would have achieved equal eminence in the Himalaya, too. But in May 1955, during the first Kenya Himalaya expedition, Firmin was killed as he descended 25,895-foot-high Himalchuli. On Mount Kenya, he's remembered by Firmin Col, just above Point Piggott, and the daunting 16,555-foot-high rock pinnacle, Firmin Tower, which lies on the north face of Batian.

By the middle of the century, fifty years after Mackinder's party reached the summit, fewer than twenty teams had succeeded in setting foot in God's Abode.

Ever defiant, *Kirinyaga* did not relinquish its sanctity without struggle. And when it did, it exacted due retribution.

Opposite: Newborn day's golden salute to the timeless majesty of Mount Kenya and its many haunting peaks. The surrealistic lenticular clouds herald blizzards to come.

# 4 Masters of the Mountain

Mount Kenya's virtual solitude came swiftly to an end with advent of the 1950s. In 1949, the peaks and moorlands above 10,000 feet were declared one of Kenya's first national parks, and roads were graded up to a height of 10,000 feet.

At the same time, the Two Tarns Hut — at a height of 14,730 feet — was built by the Mountain Club of East Africa (the Mountain Club of Kenya was established a year later) with money raised by public appeal.

The way was open. It now became possible for many to reach the moorlands with ease — and to plan expeditions that could be completed within the span of a week.

The peril of swift access to high altitude is a phenomenon acutely displayed on Mount Kenya. Standing alone, it rises out of Kenya's central highland plateau from a height of 6,000 feet — and even walking slowly from the farmsteads of Naro Moru it is possible to reach the base of its major peaks by midday of the second day, a gain of 8,000 feet in a remarkably short time.

Apart from the endemic pulmonary and cerebral oedema caused by sudden ascent to heights of more than 14,000 feet — the mountain claims half the world's high-altitude oedema cases — Mount Kenya's fragile, unstable glaciers, and sheer faces also pose a constant threat to even the most experienced climbers.

In particular, hanging in the broad wall that divides Batian's West Ridge from the South-West Ridge, are the glassy surfaces of the Forel and Heim glaciers. The face represents a forbidding and almost impossible sheer 2,000-foot face of treacherous ice and rock. Deadly and unpredictable after hours of exposure to the Equatorial sun, ice blocks frequently break away during the late afternoon. Even during the night the sudden snapping explosions of these avalanches disturbs the sleep.

But dangers notwithstanding, the elemental challenge of Kenya continued to lure all those who saw it. In the 1950s this climb remained the one supreme challenge left on Mount Kenya and despite the obvious risks, Bob Caulkwell, at that time perhaps the most powerful climber on the mountain, decided in January 1955 to pioneer the first ascent of Batian by its west face. He chose Gerald Rose as his partner.

'Everyone,' wrote Bob Caulkwell, 'who has sat at Two Tarn Hut and looked at the peaks of Mount Kenya must have admired the breathtaking sweep of the West Face. Two thousand feet of it, from the sharp point of Batian to the jumbled mass of the Tyndall Glacier.'

When Caulkwell first saw it in January 1952 he couldn't take his eyes off this, the most challenging face on the mountain: a supreme test of skill and courage, and one of the most dramatic climbs anywhere in the world. It beckoned like a siren.

Three years later, in darkness, at 5.00 am, on 7 January, 1955, he and Rose began a monumental struggle up this virtual wall of ice, reaching the summit of Batian only after thirteen hours of stamina-sapping climbing as darkness approached again — at 6.45 pm. 'The standard . . . had been unrelentingly severe

Previous pages: Porters and climbers trek across the snow line on the descent from Point Lenana to Chogoria.

Right: Mist shrouds the shelter of the Austrian Hut built to commemorate the dramatic 1970 rescue of Austrian Gert Judmaier.

Right: Top Hut latrine stands in splendid isolation among the snow-dusted volcanic rocks of Point Lenana's slopes, near the Curling Pond.

103

Opposite: Porters and climbers prepare to leave the shelter of Mintos Hut for an early morning rendezvous with sunrise over Point Lenana.

Opposite: Above the Lewis Glacier on the final stages of the approach to Point Lenana.

Overleaf: Climber beneath Point Lenana surveys the descent past the Hanging Tarn (right) and Hall Tarns (extreme left) to Lake Michaelson which lies deep below the head of the Gorges Valley. The distinctive Giant's Billard Table, a parasitical crater background), is one of the outstanding features of the fascinating eastern moorlands.

with substantial stretches of very severe.'

They had gone from the Tyndall Glacier and up the precipitous Heim and Forel Glaciers that hang precariously from the face to join the west ridge just below Batian. But they found that their way across the 'Gate of Mists' was blocked by impassable cornices. Now they had to crampon down to the steep wall of the Diamond Glacier and follow the route Mackinder took in 1899, and Firmin and Bagenal in 1950, before rejoining the ordinary route below Shipton's Notch.

So tired were the two, and so anxious to begin their descent before full darkness, that they scribbled the wrong date on the paper with their signatures which they placed in the De Reske cigarette tin that was kept on top for that purpose.

'We had expected to be benighted and had organised the trip with a view to using the near-full moon to descend by. True, we had hoped to be further on than the summit by nightfall, but we were not worried as we had plenty of warm clothes should we eventually be forced to stop.'

Steadily and cautiously they moved down the Diamond Glacier, along the ice and rock rib that divides it from the snowfield in the amphitheatre below Nelion, and on to a ledge in the shelter of the south-east ridge.

Now they moved onto the south-east face and met the full force of the freezing night wind as they abseiled down to a large, comfortable-looking ledge. 'While we were looking around for a belay, the ledge suddenly split away from the mountainside, and threw Gerald over backwards, in a shower of debris down the cliff.' Inexplicably, and unaccountably to Caulkwell, the spot where he stood remained firm.

Rose fell 300 feet before he was brought up short on a narrow ledge. Caulkwell, alone, produced some superlative climbing — described by his Mountain Club of Kenya colleagues as a *tour de force* — to reach his colleague but he was unconscious, 'very badly hurt, and certainly beyond my help'.

Caulkwell remained with him an hour or two but Rose never recovered consciousness and his partner went on down to the foot of the climb and then ran, stumbled, and hopped something like the remaining twenty-six kilometres of the mountain to raise the alarm and guide help back. But it was too late. The extent of Rose's injuries and the extreme cold proved too much. When the rescue party reached him he was already dead. Impossible to remove his body and carry it down the mountain, he was buried where he lay.

In hindsight, what is surprising is that Caulkwell and Rose were on the mountain at all. The declaration of a State of Emergency by the colonial governor in 1952, following the midnight arrest of Mzee Jomo Kenyatta at his Gatundu home, on 22 October, had added a new peril to the many that already existed.

From 1952, as British military patrols swept the forests and moorlands hoping to flush out the freedom fighters of the Mau Mau movement, the mountain was virtually sealed.

Nonetheless, the freedom struggle did have one positive outcome for the mountaineers. Neither the moorlands nor the mountain heights had ever been precisely surveyed. Indeed, when the 1950s dawned Batian was shown on official and unofficial maps as standing at between 17,040 feet and 17,140 feet above sea level — even though the British Royal Air Force had conducted extensive aerial photography of the Aberdares and Mount Kenya, using special trigonometry cameras, three years earlier.

This had been followed by a ground survey in January 1950 when a surveyor with the Directorate of Colonial Surveys (forerunner of the Kenya Survey Department), C. G. T. Bere, set off up the Nanyuki track to spend three weeks above 11,500 feet on the Kenya moorlands. Using mules as pack beasts, Bere carried both theodolite and heliograph on to the minor peaks that he used as trigonometry stations as he worked his way around the western face of the mountain. The following month his colleague, P. J. Taylor, repeated the assignment, this time surveying the east face of the mountain.

Working with each of them, on the plains below, was another team — consisting of a surveyor and heliomen manning existing triangulation points — which communicated with the men on the mountain by morse using the heliographs.

The mapping work, which had been shouldered aside by urgent development areas elsewhere in Kenya, suddenly assumed priority. When the Emergency was declared it was suddenly realised that the security forces needed these maps to enable them to carve roads through the forests to the moorlands to help them hunt the freedom fighters who used the area as their headquarters and base camps.

Even so, the sacred peaks continued to beckon, their challenge undeniable, their allure often fatal. The adjutant of one British battalion serving in the fight against the Mau Mau, used the time on moorlands patrol to launch an assault on Batian — only to die in the attempt. Another climbing party, walking in from Meru undetected by either the patrols or the Mau Mau, reached the summit. The rush was beginning.

J. W. Howard, Firmin's partner on only the second ascent of the West ridge in 1948, in a brief history of climbing on Mount Kenya published in the 1955 *Alpine Journal*, which drew attention to the remarkable record of Arthur Firmin, pointed out that by 1955 Batian had been climbed nineteen times and Nelion thirty times; some of these last ascents, of course, were made *en route* to Batian.

Of these, Firmin made no less than five ascents of Batian since he first went to the mountain in 1943, and 'he has climbed the peak by every route so far known, except the West face, including three new routes'.

Most of the secondary peaks, Howard noted, had also been climbed for the second time: Point Peter in 1945; Point John in 1946; Point Piggott in 1948; and Midget Peak — 'the most difficult of all' — in 1951. 'Most . . . have been climbed several time since then, and the era of exciting discoveries of Brand's essence and bottles of Bouvier . . . is over.'

No longer was the challenge to conquer or to explore. Now the way to 'God's Mountain's' was open to all eager enough to undertake the gruelling walk to the foot of the peaks and strong and capable enough to tackle the grades four to six — severe to very severe and sometimes extraordinary — climbs.

Howard's sense of disappointment at the lack of challenge remaining was as evident as his regret that the roads had also brought Mount Kenya's solitude to an end. He feared its pristine forests and moorlands would become too popular.

'As a result,' wrote Howard,' . . . the day's march through the forest may now be a thing of the past; but, mercifully, it will be difficult to push roads further than this . . . .'

But his fears were soon realised. Using the roads built to aid the military in their campaign against the freedom fighters, climbing enthusiasts began to develop the high areas — building more huts in which to shelter before launching their attempts on the twin peaks.

The first project involved building a memorial to Arthur Firmin — a new hut close to the Lewis Glacier, alongside the one built so long ago by Eric Carr. Paid for by funds raised in an appeal, the specially-designed, prefabricated hut was dismantled and loaded on mules for the journey up the mountain.

Three men were in charge of the building, together with other Mountain Club volunteers. Working long hours at high-altitude in freezing temperatures, nonetheless they all enjoyed their prolonged stay just below Point Lenana — making a big joke out of the fact that they forgot to carry a ladder with them to fix the roof (they could not have known of the one Melhuish and Dutton had abandoned in 1926).

'This was pointed out to Sully [a volunteer carpenter] . . . and he was asked, politely at first, to make one. He retorted that the only suitable timber being the base of the hut and he being only a carpenter, not a well-described conjuror, now was their chance to practice low level climbing. He resisted threats and entreaties . . . leaving the patient roofers to clamber up through a decreasing space and slide off an increasing area of roof.

'Perhaps it was the thought of having to help carry them down the mountain if they fell off once too often that made him relent, for the next morning he produced to a shuddering audience a contraption of nails and faith drunkenly resembling a ladder. . . .'

Up to the end of this era, the history of 'God's Mountain' remained substantially one of European conquest and discovery but even as the Mau Mau struggle began to cool and hopes of Independence grew, the challenge of nationalism began to stir pride and inspire ambition in the Africans who, perhaps, loved their mountain more than any white man.

Kisoi Munyao was destined to become the symbol of all those aspirations and long-yearned for hopes to many when, in January 1959 — sixty years after

Opposite: Mist descends over Mount Kenya's minor peaks with sinister speed, an additional hazard for climbers.

Opposite: Posts mark the
escent through the snow line
from Point Lenana to Chogoria.

Mackinder — he made the first known ascent of Batian by a Kenyan African. It was a timely achievement. For almost five years later, it was Kisoi, accompanied by other members of the Mountain Club of Kenya, including Robert Chambers and John Hull, who raised the black, green, red, and white flag of the new-born nation on the summit of Nelion at the stroke of midnight on 11-12 December 1963.

It should have flown over Batian but by the time the team reached Nelion on 11 December night was closing. It was 5.40 pm. 'Batian cleared and looked tantalisingly close,' writes Chambers. 'It was very tempting. But the decision was inevitable. . . . we could not expect to complete the crossing to Batian in less than a further four [hours]. We had just over an hour of daylight left, and it seemed that if we set out we would be both irresponsible and condemning the climax of the operation to a flag-raising in the Gate of the Mists. . . .

'We were forced to recognise that we could not safely reach Batian. Kisoi put up the flagpole, and we tried to prepare a comfortable site just below the summit.'

Towards midnight the skies cleared and already, over Embu and Meru, the party could see the celebration bonfires that had been lit everywhere in anticipation of Kenya's birth as a free nation. 'It was difficult to realise what was happening. We were afraid of falling asleep, and it was a relief when ten minutes to midnight came and we got out of our bags to get ready.

'On Nelion we were a few seconds late while we remembered our crash course on flare lighting. Kisoi raised the flag and Dennis and I took cine and photographed. We all shouted "Harambee" [Kenya's national motto meaning "Pull together"], hoping the Lenana party would hear. . . . We slept well.'

As the frost-covered flag stirred in the dawn breeze, herald of this new, proud independent nation, the team woke to the drone of a light aircraft, but shrouded in cloud they could not see it. Then, briefly, the cloud cleared and the plane came into view. It belonged to the Kenya Police Air Wing. Chambers remembers that he wept with emotion. Now the plane, piloted by Punch Bearcroft, with Charles Richards, came down low close to the team and, half stalling, drifted through the Gate of the Mists, Kisoi and his colleagues on the summit waving furiously. 'At last we realised we must hurry down.

'Kisoi was to be flown off the mountain to the day's celebrations at the stadium in Nairobi where he would be presented to Prime Minister Mzee Jomo Kenyatta.

'Kisoi was first off [the last abseil], and then he was running across the Lewis and I was shouting "Stop, stop! Wait for the film! Kisoi, wait for the film". We met on the glacier and sorted things out in haste, sitting on the snow with the sun eating into us. I wrote a message to the Prime Minister and Kisoi took that and the films.'

Three pickup points had been chosen for the helicopter but the first two — Naro Moru Tarn and Teleki Hut — were sealed off by low cloud. To reach the stadium in time, Kisoi had to be airborne by 3.15 pm. But the last pickup point

Left: Phil Snyder leads on the final stages of the Ice Window which he pioneered in a first ascent that earned headlines across the world.

Opposite: Phil Snyder tackling the forbidding headwall of the Diamond Couloir, which he originally climbed with Kenyan park ranger Thumbi Mathenge.

Opposite: South face of Nelion from Point Lenana with the saddle of the Lewis Glacier (left), streaming south-westward, and the Gregory Glacier (right), streaming north-east.

was 2,000 feet lower and several kilometres away. The Kenyan ran like the wind, heart sinking as he approached the rain gauge on the moorlands at 12,000 feet only to see it was also shrouded in cloud.

It was a day for magic, for intervention perhaps by *Ngai* and the benevolent spirits of 'God's Mountain' for when Kisoi arrived at the gauge, the clouds cleared almost miraculously. 'Stuart Whitehead managed to nip in with his helicopter and whisk him away with a mere twenty minutes to spare.'

As the rest of the team strolled down the mountain, relaxed and happy, they listened on their portable radios to the commentary on the Independence celebrations.

'At 4.40 sharp, dead on time,' wrote Chambers, 'the helicopter roared in. The crowd rose and gave Kisoi a standing ovation as he stepped out waving his [ice] axe. He walked over to the stand and was presented to the Duke of Edinburgh, the Prime Minister, and the Governor-General [Malcolm MacDonald]. To us still on the mountain it was a happy conclusion to know that he was there.'

But the new flag flying over Nelion signalled another realisation, too. Now there appeared to be little left to achieve on Mount Kenya in terms of major firsts. Batian, Nelion, Lenana, and all the minor peaks had been conquered. In fact, the only major challenge left was the first traverse of 16,264-foot-high Point Piggott, the fourth-highest peak, Batian, Nelion, and 16,021-foot-high Point John, demanding some of the most technical climbing of all on Mount Kenya.

Thus, in March 1964, four months after Kisoi's dramatic raising of the Kenya flag, in the course of a three-day-long marathon that stretched their endurance to the limit, R. W. Baillie and T. Phillips performed this feat.

Yet, at almost every turn, there was still opportunity for the dedicated and the ambitious. If four men — Shipton, Harris, Tilman, and Firmin — had left their names engraved on Kirinyaga's eternal snows for all time in the first half of this century, three more were to do so in the second half. Between them Ian Howell, Phil Snyder, and Iain Allan have reached the summit of Africa's second-highest point, more times than any three mountaineers on any other major mountain in Africa and, perhaps the world: notching up a collective total of more than 200 ascents of Batian alone.

Ian Howell who came to Kenya in 1967 was overwhelmed by his first sight of Mount Kenya — and has remained infatuated ever since. Within two years he set about his first major climb — on 16-17 September, 1969 with R. F. Higgins — leading a new route up the north-east face of Nelion.

Since then, in partnership with both Phil Snyder, at that time an itinerant, daredevil athletic American who became warden of Mount Kenya National Park in 1971, and Iain Allan, now the most experienced professional mountain guide in Eastern Africa, Howell has pioneered some of the major climbs of both Nelion and Batian.

By the time that Howell charted his first new route, a flood tide of climbers — from all parts of the world — had begun flooding in to test themselves on this

Opposite: Climbers trudge through stamina-sapping groundsel-studded scree on the steep eastern approach to Mount Kenya's main peaks.

fascinating new territory; rock and ice on the Equator. It was a tide so swift and sudden that it swept over the meagre resources of the national parks and their personnel without notice.

For many who came were too inexperienced or too daring for their own safety. And even those who no longer found the challenge of the European Alps sufficient were sometimes caught out, either by altitude or flaws in the rock or weather. Such a man was Gert Judmaier.

In 1970, almost one year after Howell's climb with Higgins, Mount Kenya became the setting for one of the most dramatic human ordeals in mountain history — a week-long saga of endurance, adventure, sacrifice, and tragedy — with Judmaier as the major player.

Shortly after midday on 5 September, 1970, Judmaier, thirty, an Austrian doctor and his medical colleague, Oswald Ölz, reached the summit of Batian by the North Ridge. There they paused to savour their triumph and enjoy the views. It was exceptionally clear.

Then they began the descent. Some minutes later, at around 16,800 feet, not far from the summit, they reached Shipton's Notch and paused to enjoy the view again. Suddenly, the rock which Judmaier was holding broke away, hurling him dozens of feet into the abyss where his fall was broken by a narrow ledge. His right leg was badly broken, hanging on by the flesh. He was immobile.

Barely conscious, Judmaier studied his surroundings and the void at his side. Nobody, he said to himself, could reach that ledge in such a manner as to save him. It was, he thought, an impossible situation. He could only be carried down on a stretcher. Reconciling himself to death, he remembers thinking how terrible it was to die so young on 'such a wonderful day' — it was a fine, bright Saturday.

Horrified, Judmaier's companion climbed down to his injured friend: a perilous and time-consuming exercise as he clung like a fly to the vertical face on Batian's North Ridge above the north-east face. When he reached Judmaier he was grateful they had both come prepared to bivouac on the mountain.

Making his friend as comfortable as possible, aware that the sub-zero temperatures could well kill him overnight, he then prepared for his solo descent down the treacherous rock. Without a colleague at the other end of a rope, he was in grave danger of plunging into the abyss himself.

As he left, Judmaier whispered to him, 'Give my love to everyone at home.' Later he recalled, 'I couldn't think of anything else to say. I knew it was all hopeless. It's funny, but I wasn't afraid to die.

'Snow fell heavily in the afternoon after Ölz left and I felt like the last man on earth. I kept thinking of the beer gardens at home and how much I enjoyed them. Sometimes I dozed but the pain always woke me again.'

Bill Woodley, then warden of the Mount Kenya and Aberdare National Parks, heard about the tragedy after Ölz reached the base of Batian and a Rhodesian climber went to the Top Hut, raising the alarm on a solar-powered radio that

Overleaf: Golden dawn flares from the east while 16,355-foot Point Lenana and the Lewis Glacier remain shrouded in cloud.

119

Howell had installed there. Woodley immediately organised a rescue team but none of the park rangers had any experience of technical climbing and so he sent word to the Mountain Club of Kenya.

By Sunday morning he and his rangers were at the base of Batian. But it was impossible to detect Judmaier, or the ledge on which he was stranded. Ölz and the Rhodesian were already climbing and were near the top of the North Ridge when they had to descend because the Rhodesian was overcome by mountain sickness. Later that morning Woodley's team were joined by members of the Mountain Club, among them Robert Chambers.

By now Judmaier's predicament and suffering had begun to dominate the media. 'God's Mountain' had become the stage of an incredible saga and many millions of people who had heard of it only vaguely, or not at all, were suddenly aware of those ice-capped peaks on the Equator that Mackinder had conquered just seventy-one years before.

But this day all attempts to reach Judmaier failed, and that Sunday night about twenty people crowded into Kami Hut, high up the mountain's northern face beneath Point Peter, or camped outside in the freezing air.

'As I'd slept on the floor,' recalls John Temple, another member of the rescue party, 'I thought it politic to get up early. I cooked some sausages and offered them round. They were not appreciated so Oswald Ölz and I ate them.' Chambers, stricken by a bout of altitude sickness, vomited outside the hut.

Temple, who was allocated to Rescue Team Two, was one of those who had answered Woodley's summons for help although he had done no serious climbing for ten years. But he was fit. A walk on Mount Kenya's moorlands a week earlier meant that he was also acclimatized.

Begging dry clothes from Temple, Ölz was determined to take any risks in the attempt to rescue his friend which impressed Temple. After changing into the climbing gear lent to him by Temple, the Austrian, with another member of the Mountain Club, Sylvano Barusso, climbed back with medicine and bandages to comfort his friend. They were followed by Temple and Luther with the Cacolet-carrying harness.

The two parties climbed all day Monday, bivouacking overnight, and it was mid-morning on Tuesday by the time they reached Judmaier. Despite the unfolding drama, Temple found the climbing 'very enjoyable'.

Now began the business of endeavouring to bring him down. The air was painfully thin, the ledge on which the victim lay under a metre wide. 'We got him into the contraption,' Temple recalls, 'and moved him down a little.' But Judmaier, his foot dangling loose, swinging from the broken bone that showed through his shin, found the pain unbearable.

'[He] quietly explained that he would rather die where he was,' recalls Temple. Unless he was anaesthetised and his legs given support, it was impossible for Judmaier to be carried down in that manner. Abandoning the attempt, they made him as comfortable as possible.

Opposite: Icicles at the entrance to a crevasse on the Lewis Glacier mark the spot where Phil Snyder, skiing down the glacier in a white-out, crashed and chipped one of his vertebrae, narrowly escaping permanent paralysis.

Opposite: Climbing party
approach the upper Teleki
Valley on the ascent from Naro
Moru.

Above: Rock hyrax have
evolved into a distinctive
subspecies in the rarefied air of
Mount Kenya above 14,000 feet.

On his way down with Pradeep, another member of the rescue team, Temple passed Dick Cooper and a reinvigorated Chambers who were carrying more medical supplies for the injured climber.

That night, Tuesday, well above 16,000 feet, Judmaier had been trapped in his icy prison for four nights. Next morning rescue seemed impossible. Impenetrable mist clothed the mountain. Nonetheless, Jim Hastings, a helicopter pilot based at Wilson Airport, Nairobi, was determined to try.

Early that morning, despite the barrier of fog and mist, Hastings manoeuvred through brief breaks in the cloud, heart-stoppingly close to Batian's massive cliffs and glaciers.

'We could hear the heavy throb of the helicopter,' recalls Temple. But he could not see it. 'Then a crash. Then silence.'

Jim Hastings had made the supreme sacrifice. Barely conscious, fast fading, Judmaier was able to understand that this man, unknown to him, had striven valiantly and fatally to pluck him from the narrow, ice-bound ledge that was his prison.

Though Judmaier was condemned to spend yet another night on the mountain, there can be no doubt that he was sustained by this knowledge — and in it found the strength and courage himself to cling to life, even though he was considerably weakened by unbearable pain, little food, and constant exposure to sub-zero temperatures.

All through the following day, Thursday, even as a team of Austrian mountain rescue experts, collected together through the efforts of his father in Vienna, boarded a plane in Frankfurt and flew out to Kenya, Judmaier clung to the fragile hope of rescue.

Indeed, at around the time the rescue team landed in Nairobi, the rescuers already on the mountain had reached Judmaier with a more comfortable stretcher. And, even though the slightest movement caused him to blackout momentarily, his helpers slowly manoeuvred him into the stretcher.

By 1.00 pm, Ölz, Temple, Chambers, and Cooper — each heedless of their own lives — began the long afternoon struggle to carry the critically-injured climber from his dangerous eyrie across the sheer precipice to a bivouac site at the junction of Batian's north and west ridges.

'We were now in a position,' recalls Temple, 'to lower the stretcher and knew the Austrian rescue team was on its way.' By the time they completed their task it was nightfall: Judmaier's sixth night on the mountain.

The following day, Friday, when the Austrians arrived just after midday — from Innsbruck it had taken them just forty-eight hours — the Kenya team carrying Judmaier were already on the ridge above Firmin Tower, at about 16,600 feet.

'We thankfully handed over to them. . . . By 10.00 pm, they had got him to the foot of the climb and by midnight to Kami Hut.' It was from there next morning the following day, Saturday, that Judmaier was flown to Nanyuki Hospital. (Ian

Makinnon, a British soldier taking part in a training exercise on the mountain much later in the 1970s was not so lucky. He fell to his death near the top of Nelion, down a 2,000 foot ice gulley now known as 'Mackinnon's Coulour' and lies buried at its base.)

The seven-day rescue operation was one of the longest and most dramatic in the annals of mountaineering history and in appreciation of the many sacrifices made and the great risks taken, the Austrian Government later provided funds and training to establish Mount Kenya's first official mountain rescue team.

Under Snyder's leadership the Kenyan rangers became consummate mountaineers and, as part of their ongoing training, also helped to establish several new routes on Mount Kenya.

These, and the routes Howell and Allan pioneered, count among the eighteen major climbing routes established in the 1970s and early 1980s by this accomplished trio so that in the 1980s, says Howell, Mount Kenya could boast the highest concentration of hard technical climbs anywhere in the world at such an altitude. Altogether, there are thirty-four such climbs of which only one or two are rated grade four, the rest all being grades five or six.

Established by Eric Shipton, one of the greatest mountain climber-adventurers of his time, as one of the great tests for severe and very severe ice and rock climbs at extreme altitudes, Mount Kenya's reputation was thus secured.

Indeed, one of Howell's climbing achievements must rank as unique in climbing history. It followed a suggestion from Mackinder, the original conqueror of Batian, in a 1930 article in the *Geographical Journal* when he proposed that a hut should be built on the summit of Nelion where climbers could bivouac overnight to rest before the dangers of descent, or the final challenge of the ascent to Batian.

Although the idea was often discussed in the years that followed, the demands and risks involved deterred anyone from attempting it.

But Howell, after experiencing the two coldest bivouacs he could ever remember on Mount Kenya, became fixed on the idea of making Mackinder's suggestion a reality. He designed a small prefabricated hut which was made in Isiolo, the scorched 'capital' of Kenya's northern desert regions at the northern foot of the mountain.

Then all that remained was to transport it up the mountain and set it in place on a narrow ice-bound ridge some 17,000 feet above the Equator. Arranging airlifts to drop the prefabricated sections on to the Lewis Glacier was easy enough. But then, 'due to [the] non-availability of useful helpers, the onerous task of carrying all the parts from the glacier to the summit of Nelion,' writes Howell, 'fell on me alone.

'The mental strain and constant concentration necessary when climbing solo began to tell. Loads were often awkward and rarely light, the rocks frequently wet and sometimes covered with snow.'

Howell finally accomplished this phenomenal task — in thirteen solo ascents,

Opposite: Snow-dusted scree marks the final approach from Chogoria.

Opposite: Duncan Karinga of the Mount Kenya Rescue Team abseiling down the glacial-polished wall of Point Piggott above the Tyndall Glacier.

Right: Ascending the West Ridge which, for Eric Shipton, the famous Himalayan climber, was the ultimate challenge on Mount Kenya. He declared it one of the most difficult climbs he had ever achieved.

Above: Skull of over one of sixty victims Mount Kenya has claimed in the last fifty years.

laden with heavy building material, of 17,022-foot-high Nelion. Since it was completed the hut has proved a godsend to almost everyone who climbs Nelion or Batian, for weather changes on Mount Kenya's summit are abrupt and without warning. Fine, clear skies give way in seconds to howling blizzards and thick mists.

The first huts on Mount Kenya were those built by Ernest Carr in the 1920s. If fortune had been more favourable those built since would account for a small-sized village.

One hut, airlifted into the Teleki Valley, could not be found and was lost for years until Park Rangers discovered it lying hidden in clumps of tussock grass on a hillside — just a few hundred metres from the spot where it was to have been built.

And the Firmin Memorial Hut was razed when a climbing party of youths lit a fire on its wooden floor. In February 1973, not long after Howell's achievement, the newly-completed Austrian Hut — a gift from the grateful Austrians to replace the Firmin Hut — was officially opened.

Considering the altitude — close to 16,000 feet — a fantastic number of guests, 'seventy or perhaps even eighty' according to the Mountain Club of Kenya's account, assembled for the opening ceremony. All had to wait for the Club's official representatives to descend Batian and Nelion.

After a brisk stumble across the Lewis Glacier, one of them recalls, 'I approached the Hut at twenty to twelve with the uncomfortable feeling that while I might be twenty minutes early, I could equally well be forty minutes late as I could not remember whether the ceremony was scheduled for 11.00 am, or noon. There was also the trousers problem. The only backside in my trousers was mine and even that was only in place'.

Duly recovered, he gave a speech thanking all concerned and was followed in turn by other officials of the club, warden Phil Snyder, and one of the rangers.

Then the the MCK plaque on the hut was unveiled and the hut was officially open 'for the use of mountaineers of all nations'.

Some months later the hut was used by Snyder and his mountain rescue team when the warden determined to mark Kenya's first decade of freedom — 12 December, 1973 — by finally raising the national flag on the summit of Batian at midnight.

He was determined not to be stalled, like the party that set out to mark the first seconds of Independence, on Nelion and for several days he and his team moved their equipment — and masses of pyrotechnics from the Kenyan Army — to the base of the climb.

Then, two days before, Snyder and his six top climbers made preliminary ascents to deposit the flag and flares on Batian in readiness for the golden moment. Another section of his mountain team made similar preparations on Point Lenana.

The team were at the top before sundown on the night of 11 December and

Opposite: Climbers pause to admire the panorama of rolling alpine moorlands where they sweep westward towards the arid Laikipia Plains far below.

Left: Weathered timber cross in the shadows of Batian and Nelion marks the lonely, rocky grave of a climber — one of many that Mount Kenya has claimed.

fortunately the night was clear and sharp. Snyder had liaised with the celebration committees all around the mountain who were waiting for the fireworks on the summit as the signal to start their own fireworks and bonfires.

'We had a great number of flares,' Snyder recalls. 'And exactly at midnight we raised the Kenyan flag as my team on Batian and the other team on Lenana began setting everything off.

'It really was a celebration. The whole sky was lit up. I could see every detail of Batian and Nelion. And then below, the plains all around the mountain came to life as townsfolk and villagers lit their bonfires and sent their fireworks into the sky.'

Overleaf: Stormy clouds at sunrise shroud the lower valleys of Mount Kenya.

Opposite: Climbers negotiate a rocky path beneath the craggy ridges of one of Mount Kenya's many radial valleys on the way to Point Darwin.

Above: Climber's camp amid the groundsel on the shores of Kami Tarn at the head of Mackinder Valley.

While Snyder and his men had to endure the bitter cold in a bivouac on Batian, the team on Lenana were more fortunate — they could use the new Austrian Hut.

Fifteen years later, as Kenya marked its twenty-fifth anniversary of freedom in 1988, it was still in use: a welcome haven for all those aspiring to set foot on the pinnacle of the Equator, rightly regarded as the most perfect model of an Equatorial mountain and in height equalled or superseded only by the Equatorial peaks of the Andes far away on the other side of the world.

And if not the highest, few mountains anywhere, if any, can challenge Mount Kenya for its wealth of contrasts: in its landscapes of forest and moorland, the richness of its flowers and plants, and the magnificence of the animals and birds that live in its forests and on its moorlands.

# 5 On God's Mountain

The suddenness of day in Africa brings a perceptive quickening of the pulse. Nowhere more so than beneath Mount Kenya's massive girth, where its rumpled flanks, deeply cut gorges, valleys, and ravines, straddle the Equator in solitary majesty.

From the north, where it rises, virtually sheer, more than 13,000 feet out of the scorching desert in less than seventy kilometres, the enormity of its bulk is difficult to comprehend — yet it is always breathtaking, especially in silhouette, backlit by the pale blush of dawn.

Slowly the first fingers of molten light grasp the sacred peaks with knuckles of gold and then the sun explodes above it in a burst of liquescent fire.

Now lambent dawn floods the forests and plains below, flushing the cold shadows of night from the thickets. As the mists begin to melt, the sun chases them along the hidden rills and ravines and across the tawny grasslands as it climbs agile above the curve of the Equator.

Only in the west, where it is hidden by the brooding 13,000-foot-high wall of the Aberdare massif, is Mount Kenya's dramatic conquest of the African plains in any way muted.

Yet even when you take the dirt road eastwards from Naro Moru on the western slopes of *Kere-Nyaga* and head straight for the necklace of snow and ice that clasps its slender throat some 10,000 feet above, glistening and sparkling in the early morning sunshine, the spectacle still draws your breath.

On a clear day, from this height, 6,500 feet above sea level, the twin peaks of Batian and Nelion seem to rise incredibly high into the startling blue of the Equatorial sky — only thirty-two kilometres away as the crow flies. From this point, the base of the peaks at around 15,000 feet, is only two days walk.

The first day takes you along the graded road that winds through the smallholdings and the lower forests, through the park gate at 8,000 feet, up to the met station at 10,000 feet.

Although this twenty-six-kilometre-long stroll is ideal for acclimatization, many choose to drive straight to the met station to begin their climb and thus miss the glories of the wildlife to be enjoyed among the stillness of the bamboo, forest, and rushing streams, that make this one of the most rewarding nature walks in Kenya. Often, those who forego the first day's trek also find themselves ill-prepared for the rigours and dangers of sudden ascent to high-altitude.

In very few places else in the world is it possible to climb to 15,000 feet in a comfortable day's walking — and this alone precipitates the onset of mountain sickness and the potentially fatal oedemas endemic to Mount Kenya.

Nor should it be forgotten that the moorlands that extend virtually up to the base of the final 2,000 feet are at much the same height as the highest point in Europe, Mont Blanc.

The remarkable contrasts that are experienced on this climb, from Equatorial African plain, through steamy bamboo belt, ancient rainforest, and mountain moorland, to permanent snow and ice, distinguish Mount Kenya from most

Previous pages: The mass of Ithinguni rises on the eastern moorlands (in background) above the Giant's Billiard Table (right). In the foreground is another parasitic crater.

Opposite: Tree groundsel, *Senecio battiscombe*, and cabbage groundsel, *Senecio keniodrendon*, stud the moorland valleys of Mount Kenya. These Equatorial mutations of tiny alpine plants reach extraordinary heights.

Opposite: Tendrils of cloud shroud majestic peaks where ostrich-plume lobelia, *Lobelia telekii,* and tree groundsel, *Senecio keniodrendron,* stand sentinel in the foreground.

Left: Few living creatures make their home above 14,000 feet, but on Mount Kenya an endemic species of rock hyrax flourishes, warmed by the Equatorial sun some 3,000 feet below the twin peaks.

other mountains, even its solitary companion, regal Kilimanjaro, some 350 kilometres distance away, which has no bamboo belt.

The mountain slopes above 10,170 feet, with their two salients — Naro Moru and Sirimon, which reach down to about 8,500 feet — were declared a National Park in 1949. The lower area, between 5,250 and 10,500 feet, constitutes the 1,420-square-kilometre Mount Kenya Forest Reserve. Along with this reserve, the 717-square-kilometre park was accepted as a UNESCO-designated Biosphere Reserve in April 1978 for Mount Kenya plays a crucial role in the life of the country. It is Kenya's single, most important catchment and its largest forest reserve. The fertile loams of its lower slopes, particularly in the north-east, sustain the growth of the nation's richest farmlands.

Five important towns, their economy dependent on the mountain farmlands, flourish and grow apace on Mount Kenya's lower slopes — including the

Overleaf: Tree groundsel and ostrich-plume lobelia stud the shores of Kami Tarn on the northern slopes above Nanyuki.

Left: One of Mount Kenya's most outstanding species of everlasting flower, *Helichrysum brownei*, common throughout the alpine moorlands of the mountain.

central highlands 'capital' of Nyeri, neighbouring Karatina, Embu, in the south-east, prosperous Meru, one of the nation's fastest growing municipalities, in the north-east, and Nanyuki in the north-west. Other important centres are Kerugoya, Chogoria, Timau, Naro Moru, and Kiganjo.

For some — Naro Moru, Nanyuki, and Embu, in particular — the tourism inspired by the mountain is as important to their economies as agriculture. Indeed, Naro Moru is the headquarters of one of only two professional mountain guides and porters organisations in Kenya — a co-operative of more than 100 members. The other is at Mutindwa, near Chogoria.

Much of the vegetation is unique — thirteen species are endemic only to Mount Kenya. Vegetation varies with altitude and rainfall and includes rich alpine and sub-alpine flora with montane and bamboo forests, moorlands, and tundra.

Right: Fading bloom of Mount Kenya's cabbage groundsel, which only flowers every twenty years or so, with giant heath, *Erica arborea* (background), and the shadowy massif of the Aberdare mountains (far background).

The western and northern forests are comparatively dry and less prolific. But in the east and to the south, where the rains are frequent and heavy, the forests are thick and rich, particularly in the number of species of indigenous trees.

In these ancient forests black and white colobus monkeys leap from one branch to another in the canopy trees. Few sights are more graceful than the colobus in flight. Below, buffalo wander through the tangled thickets. Other wildlife includes elephant, black rhino, giant forest hog, tree hyrax, white-tailed mongoose, suni, duiker, leopard, bushbuck, waterbuck, bush pig, giant rat, lion, Sykes monkey, baboon, porcupine, zorilla, and many other species.

The forests and moorlands are a treasury of many unique species of plants and trees that grow nowhere else. One of Kenya's most valuable indigenous trees, the camphor, *Ocotea usambarensis*, rises up to 150 feet high to a widespread crown and scabrous russet bark.

Left: Teleki Lodge at 14,200 feet in the Teleki Valley with (background, left to right) 17,058-foot Batian, 17,036-foot Nelion, 15,857-foot Point John, and the Lewis Glacier.

Juniper and podocarpus, two more giants of the forest, flourish in the drier parts below 8,200 feet, where the average annual rainfall ranges between 875 and 1,400 millimetres. Their massive trunks, thrusting high into the canopy, are carved by age and parasites into exotic, fluted shapes, knitted together with lianas and vines.

Higher up, where annual rainfall is more than 2,000 millimetres, bamboo dominates the contour lines between 8,500 and 9,000 feet, buffered by stands of podocarpus between 8,000 and 10,000 feet. Towards the west and north, the bamboo is smaller and less dominant.

Between 9,000 and 11,500 feet, where the yearly rainfall can exceed 2,400 millimetres, the forest is less dense and long-living hagenia is the dominant tree.

Beyond 10,000 feet, as the cold becomes more extreme, the trees decline. Podocarpus is replaced by hypericum and hagenia, which have a more open canopy and more developed understorey, and grassy glades are common, especially on ridges.

Right: Rutted murram road leads through the Chogoria rainforest to 10,500-foot Urumandi Lodge.

Right: Four-wheel drive vehicle helps haul a bogged down Land Rover on the road to Urumandi.

Overleaf: Mirror-like waters of one of the Hall Tarns, near Mintos Hut atop the cliffs of the Gorges Valley, reflect a ring of impressive peaks including (right of centre) the snowless north face of Batian and Nelion.

In the glades beneath the middle canopy the profusion of shrubs, including some members of *Rubicae* (the coffee family), is thick and tangled. They rise as high as thirty to forty feet, and the air is filled with the sweet, fragrant breath of their flowers.

The trees are host to flowering climbers such as a rare begonia, *Begonia meyeri-johannis*, with its striking, asymmetric leaves and delicate white flowers that glow softly pink.

Underfoot, the forest floor is thick with rotting leaves, ferns and occasional plants, including the balsam "touch-me-not", *Impatieus fisheri*. In bloom, this plant bears remarkable scarlet flowers with spurred edges.

Among the ferns on the valley floor and by the banks of streams, where the forest is wettest, you may come across the tall, prickly-stemmed tree fern, *Cyathea manniana*, though it is not prolific. A smaller fern, *Asplenium hypomelas*, found in leaf scars and also around the base of the forest giants, is closely associated with *Cyathea*.

Many of the marvellous birds you may see flitting through these forests are either rare or endemic, including a remarkable green ibis, the glorious Ayre's hawk eagle, the threatened Abyssinian long-eared owl, scaly francolin, Ruppell's robin-chat, and a scintillation of many different species of sunbird, long-crested eagle, Lammergeier, and Hartlaub's turaco.

On the high moorlands, which start beyond the forests at around 11,000 feet,

Opposite: East African redwoods, *Hagenia abyssinica*, mark the upper reaches of the Chogoria trail.

Left: Land Rover at roadhead on Mount Kenya's eastern moorlands.

Left: Supper of beans cooked over a glowing fire at Urumand Lodge.

Opposite: Early morning frost on the moorlands.

Left: Through the aeons tenacious lichens have etched surrealistic patterns in Mount Kenya's ancient rocks.

Left: Hardy lichens defy cold and rarefied air to flourish close to Mount Kenya's lofty peaks.

where fast-flowing streams, fed by the meltwaters of glaciers over many millenniums, have carved deep valleys on all sides of the mountain, there is a heath zone of *Erica arborea*, a weird-shaped bush, often as large as a tree and covered with moss and lichen.

This gives way higher up to tussock grass and a rich profusion of everlasting helichrysums, gladioli, delphiniums, and 'red-hot pokers' — a riot of unusual flora.

There the *Erica arborea* is intermingled with lobelias and groundsels, and other strange and unworldly plant forms. Enormous tussock grass, clovers, irises, larkspurs, and helichrysums of many different structures grow in unique form on the flanks of the high valleys.

Perhaps the most remarkable of all the world's alpine flora, many bloom only once in every two decades when they adorn the entire moorlands with a glorious burst of colour, luring beautiful, scarlet-tufted malachite sunbirds and others into their branches. At this altitude you may also see a rare lammergeier vulture on one of its forays from its cliffside eyrie. Other moorland birds you may see include montane francolin, Mackinder's eagle owl, and a rare — and endangered — swift.

Among these spectacular mountain plants are 'water-holding cabbages', *senecio*, and 'ostrich plume plants', lobelia, which are actually giant mutations of tiny alpine plants, there growing up to twenty foot high. When the leaves die they remain attached to the plant like an overcoat and help to keep out much of the cold.

The hairy grey leaves of lobelias, dotted with tiny blue flowers make the plant look like a grotesque furry giant, but the wrapping seals out the frost at night. Another form grows closer to the ground in the shape of a huge rosette filled with water. At night this water freezes over and the ice wards off deeper penetration of the cold, so protecting the central bud.

These plants mark the extreme range of wildlife. The only permanent residents at this altitude are augur, buzzard, leopard, dormouse, and rock hyrax, which look like overgrown guinea pigs and mainly graze on moorland grasses. You'll see this well-padded, ubiquitous species, *Procavia johnstoni mackinderi*, everywhere but it's endemic only to 'God's Mountain'. They thrive on scraps from the commercial lodge, in Mackinder Valley, and mountain camps and huts, moving with astonishing agility across the precipitous rocks. The soles of their feet have semi-elastic, 'rubber' pads which provide a sure grip on all inclines in all conditions.

Among the moorland mammals found lower down are the Mount Kenya mouse shrew and common duiker. Endemic mole-rat are common and there have been rare sightings of golden cat and an African hare that may be a subspecies endemic to the mountain. Buffalo and elephant frequently roam there, and lion are permanent residents of the upper forest and lower moorland. Eland and zebra have also been seen occasionally on the northern moorlands near the

base of the peaks at heights of around 14,000 feet.

It is these natural wonders, as much as its challenging assortment of climbs, that enrich Mount Kenya and yearly lure more and more visitors. In the early 1970s, around 5,000 visitors a year were drawn to Mount Kenya. By 1980 the number of visitors had more than doubled to 12,000.

There are six main routes up Mount Kenya. On the western side, these include the Naro Moru track, the Burguret trail, just north of Naro Moru and, beyond Nanyuki, the Sirimon and Timau tracks.

Arguably the most beautiful, enjoyable, and dramatic of all the approaches to the peaks, however, is the trail that Dutton and Melhuish, among so many, took from Chogoria, on the eastern slopes — following the course of Carr's Road.

And perhaps the toughest and most demanding, cutting as it does through the thickest and oldest of Mount Kenya's forests, is the Kamweti trail from the south.

But as more and more people enter the national park Mount Kenya's continued protection becomes vital. Trail proliferation along the Naro Moru track has already resulted in muddy swathes up to 100 metres wide in the lower alpine zone, and the destruction of an estimated ten per cent of the entire valley-bottom habitat in the upper Teleki Valley.

Initial attempts to redesign the trail system have met with limited success. Fire from humans and lightning are other threats in the dry, lower forest although recovery takes place through natural recolonization.

Nonetheless, it's astonishing that although the walk in full requires only two days, virtually everybody foregoes the pleasure of experiencing these astonishing variations, and Mount Kenya's wealth of wildlife and flora, to their fullest.

In recent years, as more and more trekkers and climbers have flocked to Mount Kenya, many young men among the local Kikuyu and Kimeru communities have become skilled guides and porters who know every centimetre of the mountain trails.

Among their own forbears and contemporaries have been mystics and religious zealots — both women and men — who, seeking communion with *Ngai*, have climbed barefoot to the summit of Batian.

In 1979, two climbers who reached Nelion met a fifty-two-year-old mystic — a barefoot, snow-haired man clutching a tattered bible and a small bag of food. He had already spent four nights on the mountain's second-highest point, sheltering at night in the Lowbonar hut erected by Ian Howell.

When Phil Snyder heard the reports he was disbelieving. 'It's impossible, ' he told pressmen following up the story. But a note from the rangers post in Teleki Valley convinced him. 'He told visitors that he had come from Meru, sent by God there to preach His word. Rangers at Teleki are still investigating.'

Another report said the man had climbed the mountain three times a year. He kept his charcoal stove and pots in the park.

By now the story had captured the imagination of the world. But Snyder had to wait to fly his light plane around the peak before he saw the man. He told

Opposite: Antiquated hot water system at Urumandi Lodge, high above Chogoria. Opposite right: Long drop at Mintos Hut 1,000 feet above the Gorges Valley.

Left: Weary climber rests by a mountain stream on Kirinyaga's upper slopes.

reporters the man was 'apparently dozing on top of the mountain'.

He added: 'Getting on the top of that peak is more difficult than any major alpine peak. This may be one of the most amazing climbs in mountaineering history. I thought it was physically impossible to do it barefoot. You need ropes, axes, warm-weather clothing, pitons. This man had nothing — only a small jacket to protect himself from the below freezing temperatures.'

Snyder, concerned for the man's welfare, sent a rescue team to escort him down. He told reporters: 'He faces an even greater impossibility in getting down off the mountain. It's impossible to make the descent over the snow and ice fields without falling. It's just impossible.'

After a few days, however, the rescue party had to abandon the search. The mystic, Ephrahim M'Ikiaria, from a small village near Meru, had eluded them and performed the second impossible feat — climbing safely down the mountain.

One of the climbers who met M'Ikiaria, Kenyan Duncan Karinga, said he was within twenty-five feet of the man. But when Karinga asked him, 'How are you my brother?' the mystic replied:

'I am not your brother. Go and find him.'

M'Ikiaria then moved swiftly behind a rock and disappeared in the mist.

The story made television and radio networks around the world. When Snyder discovered the man's identity, such was his admiration for the old man's feat he did not press charges for entering a national park without a ticket or permit to climb.

Opposite: Mintos Hut, welcome respite after the exhausting climb from Chogoria.

Opposite: Sparkling falls on the Nyamindi River, one of the major tributaries of the Tana, in the oldest and richest of Mount Kenya's ancient forests at Kamweti, on the southern slopes above Kerugoya.

Right: Some rare giant ferns and plants are endemic only to Kamweti Forest.

Others, too, have been inspired by religious power — or visions, as in the case of Muthoni of Nanyuki, or voices.

Julia Wanjiru of Nyeri, according to Philip Wangalwa, a journalist on the *Daily Nation*, Nairobi, climbed barefoot above the snowline in 1971 and was arrested by rangers on her way down. Wanjiru claimed she had been lifted to the peak by the power of *Ngai*. When she was convicted of climbing the mountain without a permit by a Nanyuki court she was placed on probation.

Few who live around the mountain — including magistrates — remain unmoved by the reverence bestowed upon it by the mountain communities.

Among the younger generation of porters and guides there is an inherent sense of awe and respect even though they climb its moorland slopes many times a year. Some have become highly-skilled alpinists, accompanying climbing parties to the summits of Batian and Nelion — and in 1989 these veteran climbers were preparing for the first indigenous Kenyan expedition to Everest, scheduled for some time in the 1990s.

Walking through the lower slopes in their knowledgeable company, brings the mountain to life in a way not possible for those who drive hurriedly up to the moorlands.

Park fees are calculated according to the number of guides and porters who

Left: Magnificent cape buffalo in the higher reaches of a Mount Kenya forest at 10,000 feet.

accompany you or your party and how many days you intend to stay in the park.

Scenically, the Chogoria track is superior to all else. It's also much longer than the Naro Moru route and it takes about three days to hike to the top.

From Chogoria village, the hamlet of Mutindwa, where you can hire guides and porters, is four kilometres up the mountain. If you are alone you will definitely need to hire a guide as you are not allowed into the park unaccompanied.

From Mutindwa it's about twenty-six kilometres to the park gate. If you intend to leave the park by another gate make sure you keep your receipts to show the rangers at the other gate.

Inside the park, close by the entrance, is Meru Mount Kenya Lodge, run by Meru County Council, which offers comfortable, reasonably priced, self-service *bandas*, huts, with roaring log fires and hot showers.

Some sixty minutes walk from the gate at 10,000 feet the Mountain Club of Kenya's Urumandi Hut established by Arthur and Carr, and shared all those years ago by such people as Carr, Dutton, Melhuish, Vivienne de Watteville, Shipton, and Harris, offers an alternative to the lodge.

From Urumandi the landscape is spectacular. The trail to Minto's hut, a stiff

Opposite: Large nocturnal bongo, a species of diminishing mountain antelope found on Mount Kenya, the Aberdares, and Cherangani mountains of Kenya. Now a threatened species, a large herd have been moved to the safety of the Mount Kenya Game Ranch, headquarters of the William Holden Wildlife Centre which commemorates the memory of the Hollywood film star by educating Kenya's youngsters about the natural legacy of their country.

Opposite: Mount Kenya's cloud-shrouded main peaks from the edge of the 1,000-foot sheer precipice above the Gorges Valley. In the background is the narrow course of the Nithi River before it enters Lake Michaelson.

Left: Trail-marking cairn on one of the main routes to the peaks of Mount Kenya.

six-hour walk, follows the crest of a long ascending ridge to the rim of the precipice that plunges a vertical 1,000 feet to the floor of the Gorges Valley.

On the other side of these sheer cliffs stands another, smaller sheet of water, Hall Tarn — it's a giddying but exhilarating experience to follow the trail along the edge of this stunning escarpment overlooking the valley that was scoured out by Mount Kenya's ancient glaciers. Ahead, the twin peaks beckon you forward.

Most people spend the night at Minto's Hut, perched above the head of the Gorges valley by three glittering tarns, overlooking the sparkling jade waters of Lake Michaelson, which spawns the Nithi River, and is surrounded by remarkable specimens of giant groundsel and lobelia.

From this spot to Point Lenana takes between three and four hours of laborious climbing. There are two routes to choose from: one leads up a ridge west to Simba Tarn, and then south around the peaks, passing Square Tarn, and climbing steeply up to the Austrian Hut by the Curling Pond.

The second route from Minto's leads up a slope of savage, loose scree in the

Overleaf: The main peaks seen from the head of the Gorges Valley on a cloudless day.

Opposite: Reflection of Mount Kenya's minor peaks in the mirror surface of Hall Tarns near Minto's Hut.

Above: Climber refreshes himself at Hall Tarns by Minto's Hut.

south, over a saddle, to the head of the Hobley Valley. Another hour of hard walking from this point takes you to the base of a ridge descending from Point Lenana, at the side of which are the Austrian and Top huts.

Many prefer to spend the night there and then make the climb to Lenana next morning to watch the sunrise.

Another route from the west follows the course of the Burguret river some eight kilometres north of Naro Moru on the Nanyuki road, through thick bamboo forest to the moorland. The trail passes some caves which served as a battle headquarters for the Mau Mau freedom fighters.

Higher up there are two huts — one near a natural salt lick at 10,000 feet which is known as Secret Valley Camp, and another at 11,500 feet known as the Highland Castle.

After the first nine kilometres through the forest reserve to the park gate at 8,650 feet, the Sirimon Route is the driest of all the major routes — almost all pure moorland. The trail starts fourteen kilometres north of Nanyuki, by the Sirimon river bridge on the Nanyuki-Meru road.

In such open country the wildlife is much more visible and there are fantastic panoramas over the northern deserts. This approach also provides perhaps the most stunning and least seen perspectives of Batian and Nelion — all the grandeur of their northern face, and the smaller, but no less dramatic minions, 15,466-foot-high Terere and 15,433-foot-high Sendeyo, named after nineteenth-century Maasai leaders.

Those climbing Point Lenana leave soon after midnight to enjoy a dawn sunup with incomparable vistas of Africa and — 320 kilometres away to the south — the vision of Kilimanjaro's disembodied ice crown floating like a halo in the sky at 19,340 feet.

It's also a good point from which to begin, and end, a circular tour of the peak area, climbing over the northern wall of Teleki Valley, above the Lodge, to Two Tarn col. Then the trail winds beneath Arthur's Seat, named after Dr. Arthur, into Hausberg Valley where the twin tarns of Hausberg and Oblong sit — jade stones set in the valley floor.

This two- to three-day circuit is a high-altitude ramble through an unspoilt wonderland of tiny, sparkling lakes, and dozens of dramatic but minor peaks that surround Batian and Nelion like loyal cohorts.

Ironically, this close to the sun, exactly on the Equator, visitors at this height risk both sunburn and frostbite. Compounded with endemic mountain sickness and the very real risk of hypothermia from extreme cold, particularly during the night, it is best to treat Mount Kenya with respect. Ever beguiling, it remains ever deceptive.

This part of the world that is closest to the sun — where its rays fall four-square on every single foot of ground — is extremely cold. Warm air is generated when the sun's rays boost atoms causing them to meet in frequent collision. These tiny explosions radiate the warmth that we feel. But where the air is thinnest, atoms are few and thus the collisions less frequent.

Paradoxically, though the air is cold, the sun's unfiltered ultraviolet rays cast their own warmth and one phenomenon everybody experiences on Mount Kenya is sudden extremes of temperature. When cloud covers the sun, temperatures fall by many degrees in a second. But the ultraviolet rays continue to pierce even the thickest cloud cover, causing severe sunburn and snowblindness.

With insufficient clothing — and even with many layers, if ventilation is inadequate — trekkers and climbers are prone to hypothermia when the body temperature becomes so low that the victim falls into a state of virtual suspended animation. They become comatose and appear dead. Dehydration, blistering, and fatigue are other major perils of prolonged existence at this altitude.

From Hausberg Valley the trail passes beneath the foot of the César and Joseph glaciers, and across 15,000-foot-high Hausberg Col beneath Point Peter, to the delightful tarns that distinguish the head of Mackinder Valley, looking up at the Northey Glacier.

Night is spent beneath a canopy of pin-sharp stars in absolute silence at Kami Hut by the two tarns, one with a lobelia and groundsel studded island. Above, silhouettes gleaming luminously in the moonlight, stand the sentinels of Terere and Sendeyo, dramatic and beautiful enough in their own right to qualify as major mountain peaks. In their shade rise strange and fluted columns of rock. Somewhere on the slopes of Sendeyo lie the remains of Icy Mike, a wandering elephant that, like Hemingway's Kilimanjaro leopard, inspires its own legend.

Herds of elephant frequently climb up to the moorlands and evidence of their visits are clear in many valleys where groves of groundsel suffer extensive damage. The tuskers knock down the trees to get at the succulent inner pulp. Lion also sometimes visit the moorlands and leopard live permanently in many of the valleys. Their tracks have been seen as high as 15,000 feet at the head of the Hinde Valley. (Phil Snyder was in Two Tarn Hut one night when one tried to find a way in and he has seen leopard on Simba Col and below Top Hut.)

In a cave in Liki North Valley, trekkers discovered the skeleton of an eland which was killed by a leopard and cached there. Snyder found the skeleton and skin of a colobus monkey at the base of Point Peter and surmised it had been dropped by one of the mountain's endemic birds of prey — a kite, buzzard, hawk, or eagle.

Smaller animals frequently seen in the alpine moorlands are bush duikers and kilpspringers which inhabit rocky outcrops. Wild dogs and jackals have also been seen around 14,000 feet. Black ducks and snipes sometimes nest on the mountain tarns or their shores.

One of the mountain's many jewel-like lakes — I do not know which — was the location for what may well have been the highest underwater exploration ever undertaken, when a group of aqualung *aficionados* lugged their compressed air cylinders up to the shores and plunged to its bottom.

# Epilogue

Early one March, five years after climbing Kilimanjaro, I set out from Naro Moru on my first climb to Mount Kenya's moorlands. From my first sight of them, so long ago in the 1960s, those alluring shoulders, sometimes brown, sometimes purple, sometimes cloaked in mist, had ever beckoned me. March is the driest time of the year, towards the climax of Kenya's hot, three-month-long dry spell that begins in January.

The first twelve kilometres or so of the walk from Naro Moru, through a quilt of peasant smallholdings filled with frayed, depressed, and retarded stalks of wilting maize and beans burnt to copper, too late to recover from the anguish of thirst, is hot and dusty.

Suddenly the road enters the dark, recessed gloom of the lower forest. A century ago ancient, indigenous giants sealed off the sky but these have been replaced with quick-growing exotic pinewoods planted by Kenya's Forestry Department.

As suddenly as we entered it, the forest ends. Now there are signs of settlement: dead stumps of hewn forest giants are surrounded by temporary mud-and-thatched rondavels and white-flowered potato fields.

Paul Wahome, my guide, assures me that the forest reserves are not being raped; that the settlers are there temporarily until a tea zone is established in this median belt between the low forest and the bamboo that separates it from the high forest.

Soon the farmlands are left behind. Already the air is keener. African buffalo, monolithic beasts so solid of shoulder and so malicious of demeanour they defy description, and so unpredictable and ferocious when aroused that they also defy provocation, graze the airstrip just before the Park gate.

The air is aromatic, sharp-scented with the sweet and sour fragrance of grasses and herbs, of game droppings and rotted compost. Beyond the gate the road cuts through the thick and ancient forest, up and down along a ridge 500 feet or so above the dank, humid, and impenetrable barrier of Mount Kenya's giant bamboo belt where streams cut the only trails.

Watching our presence from their perch with fitful care, or taking sudden flight in outrage or panic, brilliantly-coloured turacos and starlings, hornbills and orioles, sunbirds and wagtails, evoke a sense of time beginning. The stillness, lyrical in its sounds of silence, is hypnotic.

Climbing ever more steeply upwards, the road winds and swings along the meandering ridge, and the illusion that this is the world new-born, of being a participant in the moments after creation, grows.

Fleeting shadows swiftly cross our path. Above, in glorious black and white, a troop of colobus monkeys are making silent haste through the upper stories of the forest, gliding from branch to branch across an eighteen-metre-wide gap.

The forests here are as old as in the south of the mountain but of more temperate stock — thick, robust cedars, African olives, and the shaggy-barked *Podocarpus milanjianus*, some smooth and straight-limbed, rise sixty foot high wearing a dense crown of olive-green and ferns and mosses and Spanish Moss. 'Old Man's Beard', nourished by the frequent mists, drapes the higher branches with a grotesque embroidery.

From the valley below, the tinkling laughter of a fast-flowing stream filters through the thick-leaf foliage of forest grasses and sedges where creeping violets and blue-flowered peas are common. The chuckle of the stream is counterpoint to the heedless, crashing arrogance of a group of unseen buffalo — and now the loud, snapping burst of exploding bamboo shatters the silence. Wings flutter, trees rustle, and you sense the fretful neurosis of the startled, tiny diminutives of the jungle — Sykes monkeys, duikers and mongooses — hidden in the undergrowth, as they await their Armageddon. The silence that follows is more profound than any noise.

Everywhere there's a sense of expectancy, of dread — and of joy.

Beside the road, on a grassy bank beneath an old and venerable podocarpus tree, its lined and seamed trunk shafting more than 100 feet into the canopy above, Wahome and I pause to eat our picnic lunch.

I remain expectant, distracted like any city dweller by the peace and beauty of this alien world, watching a spider weave its silken strand between two spires of sere, seed-laden grass, sensing all the while the presence of the unseen crown above, and beyond, to which I aspire.

Its weight presses down from the hills above, a solid shadow of this world's birth: a crevassed, rock-hewn phantom that witnessed the fire and tempest of creation.

And in the shade I hear the echo of its many ancient tongues: the creaking of the trees, the groan of the earth, the rush of the stream, and the whisper of the wind.

Wahome and I need no conversation — he that hears these soliloquies many times a year and I, who never heard them before and may never come this way again — so that I may place these moments in those vaults of my mind where I store treasured remembrances.

Much later, in that pleasant, aching soak of exhaustion that speaks of life renewed by sudden and close acquaintance with the roots of its real existence, we cross over Percival's Bridge, built more than thirty years ago by British army engineers to honour the memory of an officer who died in Aden.

It is strong and sturdy and the bronze plaque set in its wall wears well: an apt memorial for one who loved *Kere-Nyaga* as only a climber can love a mountain.

The bridge is on a bend with a view, looking out north-west over the Laikipia Plains below, that tells you how far you have come and how high you have climbed. How swiftly in the past has that view, that I now pause to drink in so deeply, flashed by before when I was enclosed in a car.

In the thicket, two eland, largest of all Africa's antelopes, stand unmoving, like statues.

And then, late in the afternoon, as the restless trees sway one way and another

Above: Streaky seed-eater finds abundant pickings on Mount Kenya.

Above: Mountain chat, one of Mount Kenya's endemic species.

in unceasing rhythm, casting dappled shadows on the trail around one hairpin bend after another, we arrive at the open glade of the met station.

Ten thousand feet high. We have covered twenty-six kilometres and risen 3,500 feet. On the morrow, in the next twelve kilometres, we shall ascend another 5,000 feet. As I rest rejoicing, the chill of approaching sundown strikes my belly.

At the met station, it is best to take things gently and accustom yourself to the altitude. Either take a stroll a little higher or, if camping, take your tent an extra hour's climb up to the treeline, and rest there.

Standing tents can be rented at the met station if you find the basic timber *bandas*, too costly. Another good reason for making a night stop at this point is the mountain weather. After midday, it is often miserable — foggy, heavy drizzle, and almost zero visibility.

Though day fades fast in the swift shutter of Equatorial nightfall, there is a moment there when the sun hangs suspended above the brow of the Aberdares. In the lengthening shadows of the forest, a bushbuck stealthily enters the glade and pauses, head erect, tense, alert — and then takes flight.

Moments later a tiny suni antelope bounds through the clearing as a flight of banana bats swoops among the lowering gloom of the forest canopy. Suddenly, the trees are alive with sounds and fleeting visions: green parrots and ibises, francolins and pigeons.

In the night we hear the sawlike rasp of the leopard's roar against the muted thunder of a herd of buffalo chewing the grass outside Hagenia Hut. Half-awake, in those moments after midnight, the sounds of the forest are amplified by the darkness — the mocking, maniacal laughter of the spotted hyena and the panicking gallop of the bongo, a large nocturnal antelope distinguished by its red-striped flank. Later, towards dawn, the plaintive cry of the bush baby echoes with the terrifying shriek of the tree hyrax.

Soon after sunup, I duck beneath the lowered boom of the park barrier and follow the trail to the first bend. A flower of indescribable beauty, delicate pink, exquisitely-shaped, stamens like a filament of fire, stands under a tree. Its Latin name I do not know but I am told it is bottle flush, a rare work of botanical art, prelude for what is to come.

The road twists into a hairpin and the incline is incredibly steep. The gnarled, contorted limbs of the hagenia trees testify to their 200 to 300 years of existence — sentinels of this forest long before man ventured along these trails carved over the aeons by the buffalo and the elephant, the rhino and the forest hog.

Just over a century ago, when they had already experienced 36,500 dawns, the Transylvanian Count Samuel Teleki brushed beneath these same branches. The sense of wonder he must have experienced still prevails for those who follow.

Bright frost glitters in the glorious stillness of new-born day. Only the measured breathing of the climbers breaks the silence. Like everything else at this height — for instance, flying — distance is measured not by the foot or the yard or the mile but by the altitude and the hour.

Well beyond the antennae of the radio station, where the road ends, 1,000 feet above the met station, I am told it is five hours to Mackinder's Camp. Under my straining breath I estimate that it is more likely to be six or seven. Here time, too, is also comparative — measured not by the second or the minute or the hour but by the foot tread.

Along the rough trail, crouching beneath the now stunted hagenia, I finally come to a sheer step and emerge into bright sunlight. The forest ends as neatly as if it were divided by a knife. Ahead of me, appallingly steep and forbidding, rises a massive and sullen rampart that hides those glorious peaks — 1,000 feet of treachery known as the 'Vertical Bog'.

At the start of the rainy season water cascades down this fifty-five degree incline like a white-water rapid. Later, as the rains continue and the water sinks deeper beneath the surface, it becomes a waist-deep, swirling torrent, rushing soundlessly down the steep-pitched slope. What, in the dry season may take anything from ninety minutes to three hours to traverse, now becomes a day-long battle for the inexperienced.

But this is the dry season and there is no water. Perhaps this, and this alone, inspires my aching legs and labouring lungs to push on upward. But the pauses become more frequent: rest is conditioned by your breathing, not your measured step.

Undoubtedly, for botanists the longer the climb lasts the better. Almost immediately the hagenia is replaced by *Erica arborea* — a giant mutation of small alpine heather shrubs — endemic only to Mount Kenya. Higher up, following the red posts that serve as trail markers, the crest of the 'Bog' remains elusive, seemingly unattainable, as far distant as it appeared the hour before.

Now the *Erica arborea* is intermingled with lobelias and groundsels, and other strange and unworldly plant forms — enormous tussock grass, clovers and irises, larkspurs and helichrysums.

Early in the afternoon, an hour or two behind Wahome, I reach the crest of the 'Vertical Bog' and the incline slackens — still steep but not so severe. Just a few more hundred feet to a small rock bluff.

I round the corner of it and now all tiredness vanishes. Above the next crest, sharp and clear, tremendously close in the pellucid air, rise the twin peaks of Batian and Nelion.

My lunch is an orange and some stale sandwiches and a bottle of beer. Sat on top of the bluff, the moorland shoulders sweeping away on either side of me, unable to take my eyes from this vision, I munch the sandwiches.

Kilimanjaro's highest point is the rim of a volcanic crater and, close to, it lacks that perspective of scale and majesty that endows *Kere-Nyaga* with its dramatic grandeur. Mount Kenya is pure theatre, a dramatic explosion of craggy spires, a raised fist of rocky fingers.

Overwhelmed by humility and a feeling of inferiority, I turn and look back over the way that I have followed. Far below, winding out of the haze that

Opposite: Giant groundsel.

enfolds Naro Moru, I can make out the narrow ribbon that leads to the park gate 4,000 feet beneath me. To the north, Africa stretches out into infinity.

Sometime later I reach the south wall of Teleki Valley, the crest of a long radial ridge with the peaks and the grand west-facing amphitheatre visible in all their glory — no more than five kilometres distant along the trail.

The ridge looks as if it drops all the way down to the final saddle. Beyond that lies the grand arena, with *Kere-Nyaga* centre stage. It's an illusion, of course. In effect, the valley floor rises up to meet the 14,000 foot contour at the base of the peaks and, in fact, the trail actually rises another 200 or 300 feet.

By the time we cross the fast-flowing Naro Moru stream to the other side of the valley and hike the final kilometre to Teleki Lodge it is late afternoon and the mists have already begun to swirl and boil around the many spires. At the very summit a plume of cloud trails off the pyramid point of Batian as the sun's dying rays paint it a molten gold.

This recent addition to the radio station, ranger's post, and Mountain Club buildings in the valley, is certainly no five-star hotel — just a simple concrete slab and tin-roof barrack room which serves as the most common departure point for the severe walk, but nonetheless walk, up the steep-pitched scree alongside the Lewis Glacier to Lenana Point — but it does at least provide some warmth and the company of fellow climbers, Kikuyu guides, and porters.

In the morning, the sun glistens off the wall of the glacier — one of eleven remaining glaciers on the mountain, reminder that long ago, when ice covered much of Mount Kenya, the glaciers swept down below 10,000 feet. At the turn of the century there were eighteen glaciers, most of them much larger than those of today. Seven have since vanished and those that remain are shrinking fast.

Lewis Glacier, the largest and most prominent, is easily visible from a great distance, particularly during the rainy season when it is covered by fresh falls of snow. In 1899 it covered more than half a square kilometre. Now, in swift retreat, it has shrunk to much less than half that size.

So large it makes its own weather, Mount Kenya is usually clear most mornings, clouding over in the later afternoon. It has two distinct dry seasons — January to March and August to October — much in tune with Kenya's general climate. The mountain's wet seasons coincide with the country's long and short rain periods.

From Mackinder Valley the trekker who climbs Point Lenana can descend down the Chogoria route, either through Hinde Valley or Gorges Valley, by far the most dramatic with its sheer 1,000-foot-high cliffs above the cascading Vivienne Waterfalls. It marks the extremity of Carr's Road and demonstrates once again the breathtaking contrasts and scintillating loveliness of this Mountain of Mountains.

From either valley, you can explore Lake Ellis and, beyond that, the strange configuration christened the Giant's Billiard Table, and also take in the glories

183

of 12,770-foot-high Ithanguni and Lake Alice sparkling in a depression on its slopes. These lakes are sacred to the Meru people.

Trekkers who extend their stay at Minto's Hut beneath Point Lenana can also explore the southern slopes, around 16,150-foot-high Coryndon Peak, named after a 1920s South African-born British Governor of Kenya, and 15,600-foot-high Macmillan Peak.

No matter what, one thing is certain — whichever aspect of Mount Kenya they look upon they will be rewarded by one of the grandest sights in the natural world.

For many, even those without religious conviction, the sights inspire a feeling of reverence and awe. Like a worshipper in some ancient Norman edifice erected to the glory of God, you look around and realise that nothing of man can match this splendour.

In the amphitheatre at the head of the Teleki Valley the sun rises late over the serrated cliffs to the east — well after 7.30 am — when most of Kenya has been bathed by its warmth for at least an hour. Yet to thaw, an icy thread spawned in the vanishing ice of the Lewis Glacier, the Naro Moru river hangs in suspended motion. Only when the morning sun moves westward will it warm enough to free itself from its glacial prison.

During the night and early morning the winds carry a thousand howling banshees in their icy breath. But now all is still as luminous light, a light so pure that it sparkles, hangs in the air across the ice saddle that divides Batian from Nelion, pulsating, scintillating in the rarefied air.

And there, peeping almost demurely from behind, an illusion of Point Lenana.

In the shadow of the twin peaks, Point John seems to lean inward like a tower of Pisa as if about to topple on to Midget Peak which stands just beneath and between it and the base of the two great peaks.

The valley wall curves around to the edge of the barren Lewis Glacier where, now freed by the sun, the Naro Moru river leaps and bounds down the moraine.

Climbers may wish to conquer these sheer pinnacles of rock and faith but many may simply choose to rest beneath them, on the north side of this cathedral amphitheatre, as I did, and pay homage to the Creator, to *Ngai*, to the Divider of the Universe, and acknowledge man's puny scale in the perspective of nature's grand design.

Surely, here on this sacred mountain, I have walked with God.

Opposite: Waters of Lake Michaelson glisten in the early morning light, 1,000 feet beneath the Temple. In the background is the silhouette of Ithinguni.

Overleaf: Hall Tarns with Lake Michaelson at the head of the Gorges Valley below and the serrated spires of The Temple in background.

Following pages: South-east ridge of Nelion across the ice saddle of the Lewis Glacier with Lewis Tarn at its foot. Mackinder and his two Swiss companions made their first attempt on Mount Kenya along this ridge but had to turn back.

Pages 190-191: Sundown over Teleki Valley.

Page 192: On the way up.

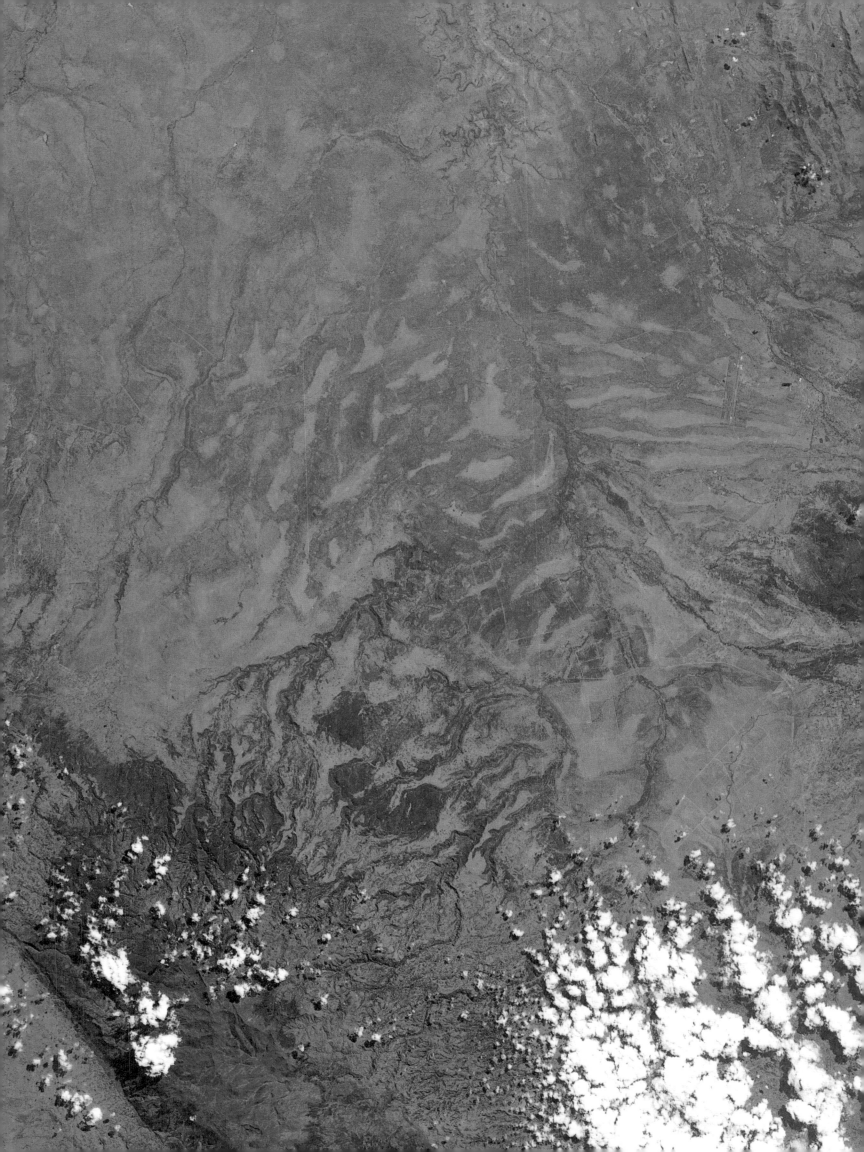